Street Theatre and Other Outdoor Performance

Bim Mason

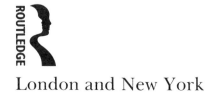

London and New York

First published 1992
by Routledge
11 New Fetter Lane, London EC4P 4EE

Simultaneously published in the USA and Canada
by Routledge
a division of Routledge, Chapman and Hall, Inc.
29 West 35th Street, New York, NY 10001

Typeset in 10 on 12 point Baskerville by
Florencetype Ltd, Kewstoke, Avon
Printed in Great Britain by
TJ Press (Padstow) Ltd, Padstow, Cornwall

British Library Cataloguing in Publication Data
A CIP catalogue record for this book is available from the British
Library

Library of Congress Cataloging in Publication Data
Mason, Bim
    Street theatre and other outdoor performance / by Bim Mason.
       p.   cm.
    Includes bibliographical references and index.
    1. Street theater.   2. Theater, Open-air.   I. Title.
PN3203.M37   1992
792'.022—dc20   91–43615

ISBN 0-415-07049-X   ISBN 0-415-07050-3 (pbk)

For Rosie

Contents

List of illustrations

All photographs by the author

Preface

This book started life when I received a bursary from the Arts Council of Great Britain to research into street theatre in the spring of 1989. The requested report grew, as whole new aspects began to open up, until it was suggested to me that I develop it into a full-length book. It has provided me with an opportunity to reflect upon the experiences of the last fourteen years and to widen my knowledge in other areas. In trying to stand apart from my own tastes and preferences I have learnt a great deal. I hope that other performers and directors, along with promoters, students and teachers, will share my enthusiasm for this most exciting area of theatre.

Acknowledgements

•

I am very grateful to all the people who have assisted in the research, writing and publication of this book, in particular Rosie Spencer, Kevin Brooking, Ralph Oswick, Brian Popay, Hilary Strong, Penny Saunders, Tim Britton, Richard and Thurzei Robinson, Chris Lynham, Patty Bee, Ross Foley, Les Sharpe, Robin Morley, Charlotte Lang, Helena Reckitt, the Arts Council of Great Britain, the Limburg Street Theatre Festival and especially Helen Crocker.

The growth of outdoor theatre

Chapter 1

The unappreciated outsider

At the end of the twentieth century, theatre is undergoing yet another transformation; while mainstream theatre is having to compete with the modern technology of film, theatre and video, there is a whole range of theatrical activity beginning to develop outside the restricting walls and conventions of traditional theatre. The borders between entertainment and art, between audience and performer and between the performance itself and the larger social event are becoming less defined. New methods are being tried out, new relationships sought. What is important about outdoor theatre is not that it has no roof over it – many of the groups described in this book also perform indoors in such spaces as old churches, warehouses, tents, museums and exhibition halls – but that it is away from the pre-defined structure of a theatre building. It has to be reinvented, often by people with no formal drama training. Within this area of work are some of the most exciting new developments in theatre, exploring possibilities that have never been foreseen.

However, there remains much prejudice in the arts establishment against these new developments. The media are much more inclined to report and review indoor theatre and the resulting low profile of outdoor theatre means that actors, orientated towards big success, will not be inclined to perform outdoors. Their attitudes reflect commonly held perceptions of street theatre – there does not seem to be a coherent new method to be studied and learnt, just a lot of untrained amateurs putting on inferior shows, often without a proper costume or character, anyway it's not acting at all and well really it's not proper theatre is it?

So outdoor theatre remains the unappreciated outsider busily getting on with its own development and expanding its popularity, with very little recognition of its work. One of the aims of this book is to show how much craft and expertise there is involved in this area of work. The vast majority of performers have received very little formal theatre training and would perhaps find it hard, themselves, to articulate their aims and methods. Also, because it is a relatively new field, most practitioners have learnt by trial and error and so have a practical approach rather than a theoretical one; they take for granted what does and what does not work. By increasing an understanding of methods and aims, this book aims to show other possibilities to practising performers and to enable them to have a perspective on their own work. I hope it will also be of use to the ever increasing number of promoters of outdoor theatre who may better determine the appropriate type of performance for their event; they may like to try less well-known forms of outdoor theatre such as journeys. They may also become more able to choose suitable locations and create the right conditions for the performers. Above all the book aims to encourage and inspire new people to the field. There is, of course, no substitute for getting out there and trying it, but they may be spared some of the trauma of that first experience of outdoor theatre. They may even get a few clues as to why a performance succeeds or fails. Because the book assumes that some readers will have little previous knowledge of the field some of the points may seem obvious or over-explained to those with greater experience.

There is such an enormous range of outdoor theatre that, for example, there seems little connection between a solo juggler performing to a small, intimate crowd and the massive, expensive, one-off spectacles performed to thousands. Because of this diversity it has been necessary to limit the scope of the book in three ways.

First, this is not intended to be a complete history or geographical survey of outdoor theatre. There has already been much published work on the commedia dell'arte, carnival, pageants, mystery plays and other old forms of theatre that took place outdoors. Some comparisons with the past are made in order to place the present situation in its historical context, but only where there is a relevant influence on the contemporary scene. For similar reasons traditional outdoor theatre in areas outside Europe is only referred to. The criteria and motivations

Figure 1 Unintended theatre in Barcelona

discussed in the book, although based in Europe, are also applicable to the USA, Japan, Australia, New Zealand and many other places outside Europe where there is a renaissance of outdoor theatre.

Secondly, it is necessary to limit the book to theatre which is intended as such. There is plenty of drama outdoors and an element of performance starts to occur if the participants become conscious of spectators and 'play up' to them. For example, the demolition of houses in Barcelona, pictured in Figure 1, was watched by a large group of locals, so the bulldozer drivers began to show off their skill with exaggerated nonchalance. Although the destruction of the neighbourhood was certainly a poignant drama it was not intended as theatre. Vociferous disputes with traffic wardens, visits by dignitaries and even weddings, contain dramas that attract the interest and even the participation of passers-by. Many outdoor theatre groups, particularly walkabout groups such as Scharlaten, Trapu Zaharra Teatro Trapero and Natural Theatre, use real-life situations as the basis for their pieces to create dramas that are at first indistinguishable from the real event. Because the events portrayed are not immediately recognisable as being artificial, the effect is much stronger. When Teatro Trapero use a real ambulance and have real medical workers rounding up a couple of actors playing escaped mental patients, they are using the strong impact created by emergency vehicles to create interest and real tension. Because of the stronger effect, the actors can be much more subtle in their actions. Also, the public can become much more animated if they believe the situation is real. The term 'Invisible Theatre' was coined by the Brazilian director Augusto Boal to describe this technique. One performance that he organised took place on a ferry-boat. An actor played a passenger who started making racist remarks about other actor/ passengers; the fact that they were actors was not made apparent until after the whole boat had become involved in the dispute. In this way, how people react can be examined – do they choose to become involved, how serious does the situation get before they take action?

Some activities such as spectator sports, political rallies and street trading, are not thought of as theatre but nevertheless are intended to have an effect on spectators, so there is an element of pre-planned performance. Interestingly, all three of these activities are increasingly introducing a theatrical element and may even engage professional performers for their event. The outer edges of theatre are likely to blur into other activities more and more in the future but this book must confine itself to the work of those whose primary intention is to present theatre.

Thirdly, the book will be dealing only with professionals and those artists who have developed their outdoor theatre work over many years. Community plays have a mix of amateur and professionals that is better dealt with by other writers, particularly since they are not always performed outside. Also, many indoor theatre groups have attempted outdoor theatre, either for advertising purposes or in order to reach a wider public. They are often surprised by their failure because they know they are quite capable as performers but they usually do not take enough account of the different criteria outside. They become frustrated at the lack of conducive conditions – a static crowd, a degree of quietness and an absence of interference by dogs, children and weather. They often seek to exclude chance factors rather than working with them, to the point at which the performance is virtually indistinguishable from what takes place indoors. In London's Regent's Park every summer, plays by Shakespeare are performed at night with lights, on a stage, with backdrop, wings and a seated audience. Although this is undeniably theatre outdoors and very professional, it is not substantially different from indoor theatre.

I have chosen to write in most detail about those performers and companies which are good examples of different types of work rather than attempting the impossible task of providing a comprehensive survey. There must be thousands of buskers (see p. 8) throughout Europe but it seems futile to go into a detailed description of too many of their shows since their aims and methods are quite similar even if the individual acts vary enormously. The amount of emphasis given in the book in no way represents the importance of each group. For example, the work of Welfare State and Odin Theatre has already been well documented so there seems little point in repeating the exercise.

Because of the breadth of the subject, it is more useful to describe types of work rather than giving in-depth profiles of a few groups. There are a vast number of practitioners at any one time and they come and go with extraordinary rapidity, so to focus only on those groups that are long-established would deny the importance of enthusiastic and original newcomers, who for one reason or another do not stay long in this field of work. Because of this rapidity of turnover, there seems little point in too much emphasis on dates; it is the nature of new developments rather than their timing that is the concern of this book. The field is so diverse that it could in no way be called a cohesive movement − some practitioners may feel they have nothing in common with others in terms either of aims and methods or of levels of professional commitment. Long-established groups may not like to be included alongside buskers, but finding dividing lines between the extremes is very difficult. Buskers gradually become well established and start to be paid by fees; better-trained and more established performers may do some busking for spare cash or for the refreshing direct contact with the audience.

The extreme diversity has made it necessary to classify the work in order to make some sense of it. This has been done in two ways. First, I look at the aims of the artists and divide them accordingly into entertainers, animators, provocateurs, communicators and performing artists (terms which will be explained later). Second, I analyse the different methods of stationary and mobile performance, and examine the logistics of various sizes and types of activity. Although this classification has been necessary, there are few clearly defined dividing lines between the different types. Most practitioners have many different aims, some do both stationary and mobile performance within one show. It is virtually impossible to find examples that are purely of one type and, as will be seen, matters of artistic taste and style vary enormously within each grouping.

Finally, in this introduction, it is necessary to explain some of the terms used throughout the book – the commonest misunderstanding being about the term 'street theatre'. In Britain this is used to describe work that may not be designed at all for the streets. The German word 'Openluchttheater' is much more appropriate. In general I have only used 'street theatre' where I specifically mean work that is designed for the streets, and not only that sort which is referred to as 'busking'. This is a word that may not be familiar to those outside Britain. Buskers are those who do shows and then collect money from the audience rather than being paid by a fee or through box-office receipts. A 'show' implies a stationary piece, whereas 'performance' denotes a much wider range of activity. Similarly, there is a difference between 'acting' and 'performing' – the former implies impersonation or artificially created emotions whereas the latter has less to do with pretending and may make more of a feature of the individual personality.

Chapter 2

Attitudes and context

CHANGING ATTITUDES

Over the last fifteen years there has been a major change in attitudes towards outdoor theatre. Even as late as the end of the 1970s, street performers were being arrested and charged with begging or obstruction. Although local authorities still try to keep a tight control on the place, timing and quality of casual buskers, many cities, particularly tourist centres, have allowed them space to perform. When the Pompidou Centre in Paris was designed to include a space specifically suitable for street entertainers a milestone was reached and other cities gradually followed suit. It became recognised that busking can improve the atmosphere of uninspiring modern shopping centres by providing something colourful, lively and out of the ordinary. Pre-arranged outdoor performances are actively encouraged and may well be paid for by local authorities. Many festivals, all over Europe, are organised exclusively for street theatre and most international cultural events have their street theatre contingent. There is an ever-increasing demand for outdoor theatre and gradually its contribution to the arts is becoming recognised. Newspapers have even begun to review outdoor theatre in the same way as they do indoor theatre, although some prejudice still remains.

The emergence of new areas of artistic activity does not happen in a vacuum. The growth of outdoor theatre in the last few years demonstrates that there was a need which it fulfils and a role that may become increasingly important in the future. This rapid development is part of the result of two great changes during the twentieth century. The first is the 'democratisation' of art, as a result of political and economic changes since the First World War, and the second the enormous transformation of the performing arts brought about by the communication technologies of film, television and video.

The effects of film, television and video

The introduction of the movies was a disaster for all those involved in the live performing arts (except for the few who were lucky enough to transfer their employment), whether they were performers, entrepreneurs, or backstage hands. The movies, once produced, had cheaper running costs; a movie house could employ fewer people and less skill than a vaudeville theatre; one product could be shown simultaneously all over the country. Because it was cheaper to run it could undercut the ticket prices of live performance and therefore the working classes began to move away from the theatres and music halls.

The dominant theatrical style at the beginning of the twentieth century was melodrama – a popular style despised by critics for being sentimental, moralistic, two-dimensional and with a lurid undercurrent of sex and violence. In fact not dissimilar to some modern movies. This style, disdained by the well-educated classes and no longer patronised by the working class, disappeared. Theatre was now to serve the more educated classes, a rut that it has failed to get out of. Television and video have further compounded this trend and, despite all the efforts to reach out to new audiences, theatre has become marginalised like poetry, opera and ballet. This is not to denigrate the quality of work or the courageous attempts by everyone in theatre to reach out to new audiences, with imaginative ticket schemes, community involvement, kitchen-sink relevance, or cosmetic inclusion of popular ingredients like circus skills.

The problem of economics remains – video libraries are now undercutting cinemas. However, this is not the only attraction of the new technologies; they are more effective at reproducing illusion; they create an illusion that requires less effort of the imagination. The result is that theatre cannot compete on the same terms. This has led to the move away from naturalism in theatre. All the trappings that created illusion – realistic sets, the lighting and stage effects – were stripped away. Brecht, in his work, prevented any possibility of the audience lapsing into the illusion that the actors were real characters. Grotowski's 'Poor Theatre' was stripped bare of inessential set and costumes in order to reinstate the actor as the dominant feature onstage. In tune with postmodernist trends, the previously hidden mechanics of theatre began to be revealed. (The architectural equivalent is the Pompidou Centre in Paris in which the water pipes, air ducts and stairs are displayed on the outside of the building.) In the theatre musicians were no longer hidden in the orchestra pit but began to be placed onstage in the manner of Asian theatre. Nowadays they are frequently included in the main action. The mechanics of changing costumes, putting on masks and creating stage effects can now be done in front of the audience. It is the ingenuity of creating pictures out of simple objects and physical skills that audiences appreciate more than the completeness of the illusion. There is a more direct and honest relationship with the audience.

It has also been realised that the great advantage that theatre has over television and film is the proximity of the audience and the possibility of interaction with them. The proximity has meant that physical skills can be appreciated better and the performer can have a greater effect on the audience. The physical theatre of Grotowski and his followers emphasised the importance of disciplined training and the involvement of the actor's whole being so that the audience witnessed the actor undergoing a total physical/spiritual experience. The possibility of interaction has meant that improvising skills and the personality of the performer become more important. This, in turn, means that the writers lose their predominance in the creation of the work.

Outdoor theatre is well placed to explore all these new developments. It has to be honest about the mechanics of its operations because, outside, less can be hidden. It must not rely on sets and lighting because it must be mobile. The difficulty of hearing text outside, means that there is more emphasis on visual image, physical skills and improvisation than on the written word. Without the defined spatial arrangements of indoor theatre all kinds of interaction with the public are possible. It can create the intimate theatre of one performer, one spectator in a confined space (the Smallest Theatre in the World which is the side-car of Marcel Steiner's motor bike), or the large-scale spectacle watched by thousands. The performers can have a greater effect on the audience because they can get amongst them, encircle them, lead them on journeys, play with them, surprise them by appearing in unexpected places, or surround them with fireworks. The widening of possibilities is creating a whole range of exciting developments.

The democratisation of art

All through the nineteenth century and into the beginning of the twentieth, artists were regarded as a special breed. Although, in theory, anyone with enough talent could make their mark, in practice, the 'lower' classes were more concerned with earning a living and lacked the education necessary to enter into intellectual and artistic circles. So artists tended to belong to the well-educated classes. Even within these classes they were seen (and saw themselves) as a world unto themselves.

In conservative late-Victorian Britain this was especially the case, but elsewhere in Europe, even the artists who were involved in revolutionary struggles saw themselves as separate from the masses they were supporting. For example, in revolutionary Russia the artists wanted to celebrate the heavy industrial machine as the saviour of mankind, the ultimate tool to liberate human beings from toil. They wanted a complete break with the old world and so rejected figurative art in favour of new abstract forms. There followed an exceptionally vital period when all kinds of experiments were made (and supported by the liberal Communism before Stalin took over). Although their creations celebrated the aspirations and tools of the New Man, they bore no relation to what the workers actually wanted. These artists saw themselves as the *cognoscenti* who would re-educate the aesthetic eye of mankind. Eventually content and accessibility were given preference over form and experimentation; Russian art became more a celebration of the hero-worker.

At the other end of the twentieth century, art is no longer the preserve of the few. This is mainly due to the demystification of art as a result of better general education. Literature, visual art, music and drama are taught in schools and there are innumerable part-time courses for older people. With the basic struggle for existence no longer such a preoccupation and increased leisure time in the wealthy democracies, more people are able to explore their artistic potential. Improved communications have opened up far wider prospects for artists to find their appropriate markets. This does not mean that there are more great artists around, just that more people can have a go. Street theatre is one of the ways people can try out performing, and is probably the best way to learn about certain aspects of it. It also provides a means of earning a living and for some it becomes a whole way of life.

Not only is there more encouragement for people to be artistically creative, there is also a much greater demand for art to be accessible to a wider public. In part this has been brought into focus by the unpopularity of modernism, which still remains incomprehensible to the vast majority. Public arts funding bodies are sensitive to the criticism that they pay vast sums to art forms which are enjoyed only by a minority. Although they continue to do so, they are more responsive, especially in more socialist countries, to the demands of popular art.

The purpose of doing theatre on the streets is to reach people who are unfamiliar with theatre, it therefore can never afford to become too elitist. Every performance must be well crafted in methods not normally thought of as art but equally as exacting, otherwise the public can simply turn their backs and walk away. Not all outdoor theatre is designed to suit everyone's taste. As will be discussed later, some groups target their work for 'arthouse' audiences or the rock music youth. However, it is also true that the vast majority of outdoor theatre is intended to be attractive and accessible to an audience far wider than those who visit indoor theatres.

THE HISTORICAL CONTEXT

The current field of outdoor theatre contains as much diversity in its aims and influences as the rest of the performing arts. On the one hand there are the popular entertainers and on the other are the artists. Even when they are brought together within the pages of *The Stage* or in this book they are awkward in each other's company. For better or worse the separation between the two is becoming increasingly indistinct as experimentation is given less room to fail by underfunded arts bodies and artists are forced to operate according to market forces. Before looking too far ahead, it will be useful to look, very briefly, at the history of these two lines of development and indicate where they have had influence on contemporary outdoor theatre.

Shamanism

The origins of the artist and the entertainer ultimately have the same root in the figure of the shaman. In primitive societies the shaman is the person responsible not only for the spiritual and physical well-being of the tribe but also for organising the rituals and dances. In central Africa today, pygmy tribes have a group of men who are given the role of 'clowns'; their leader is the shaman. Because of the relative abundance of food in the rain-forest their services as hunters are not desperately needed so they can afford to spend their time embellishing the rituals of life and death by decorating the environment and animating the dances. Many of these are light-hearted 'parties'; for example, to celebrate the successful retrieval of a hive of honey. Shamans are both artists and entertainers.

Many modern theatre practitioners have a nostalgia for theatre that still has powerful spiritual significance for the audience and performers alike; some have tried to reproduce certain aspects of it. Unfortunately, we no longer have the universally shared belief systems necessary for such a role. For some performance artists, such as Bruce and Jill Lacey who performed their ceremonies at country fairs, it is not a problem if the spectators do not see the significance of the rituals, it is the performing of the actions that counts; the spectators can make of it what they will. Others, such as Welfare State, create rituals for naming ceremonies, weddings and memorial services. Many modern avant-garde groups have been influenced by Asian ritualistic theatre, particularly that of Bali and the Japanese Noh theatre. Watching some of Grotowski's work was not unlike the witnessing of the trance state of the shaman. Grotowski's work influenced Eugenio Barba and the Odin Theatre in Denmark, a group committed to celebratory outdoor theatre and to cross-cultural exchange by 'bartering' their work for the rituals and indigenous performances of cultures far removed from their own.

Many shamanistic activities gradually lost their meaning and became more of an entertainment. We can see the relic of an ancient death and resurrection ritual in the English mummers' play, still being performed but transformed over the centuries into a comic sword fight, death and cure which is performed as 'a bit of a laugh' by the participants and received as a curious and light-hearted entertainment by the spectators. The folk theatre traditions remain as a powerful link to timeless themes and still provide a rich source of inspiration for groups such as Welfare State and Mummer & Dada.

So there is an indirect link between shamanistic practices and the work of some contemporary theatre artists. There is, however, a much more direct link between them and the skills of the entertainer.

Popular entertainment

From accounts of shamans' activities in Sierra Leone, South Africa, Alaska, Nigeria and North America it is apparent that ventriloquism, sword-swallowing, escapology, conjuring, puppetry, levitation, stunts with fire and beds of nails all have their origins in the mysterious effects created by the shaman. An example is the 'egg bag', a standard piece of magician's equipment today, which derives from the snake bag of the American Indians: two snakes are produced from an 'empty' bag (with a double lining) and are then replaced in it and 'disappear'. Even the word 'conjuring' comes from these activities, suggesting, as it does, the conjuring up of benevolent spirits in order to effect the necessary cure. It has been suggested that even acrobatic skills derive from the trance dances of the shaman.

Many of these effects would have entered Europe from Africa, the Near and Far East via the trading routes established over the centuries but especially through the invitation of bizarre acts to the courts and palaces of the aristocracy. Gradually the acts would lose their magical function and be adapted to improve their entertainment value. Peter Badejo, a well-known Nigerian dancer and choreographer, showed this process still occurring when he described bringing traditional dances to Europe. In Nigeria the dances in their rural setting retain their significance and involve long sessions of fairly repetitive dancing by the whole community. When asked to perform in Europe in front of non-participating spectators, who have no idea of the significance of the dances, he must enhance the aesthetic qualities and provide a varied programme.

Similarly in Bali, an island reeling under the effects of mass tourism, the rich tradition of religious theatre is gradually being adapted to suit the requirements of the average tourist; performances must last no longer than an hour and be at convenient regular times, proper seating must be provided and the performances are turned towards the audience as in proscenium arch theatre. Normally the theatrical rituals are performed only at certain times in the year, they may last all night or longer, no seating is provided and the dramatic enactment is as much for the participants as it is for the spectators. Indeed there will be a less clearly defined separation between the two.

So gradually the physical performing skills that we are familiar with today changed their function and became entertaining curiosities. Jugglers and acrobats can be seen in images that survive from the Babylonian, Minoan and ancient Egyptian civilisations. The Roman Empire was a particularly fertile soil for the development of this tradition with its lavish patronage of popular entertainment and its contacts with many different cultures. The rise of the Christian Church ended the encouragement of these 'frivolous' activities, which the Church actively suppressed at various stages in its history. Forced outside the main centres of civilisation, the individuals and families formed themselves into troupes that travelled around Europe leading a precarious existence. These jongleur troupes, as travellers and outsiders, were welcome only as long as they pleased and not a moment longer, so they were in a very insecure position. Today the same relationship and attitudes remain. All street performers are outsiders of one sort or another, nowadays more in terms of life-style than geography. The authorities are still slightly suspicious that there is something potentially dangerous about people not dependent on the established society and thus independent of its rules. Also, as travellers, the fear is that they could escape punishment before the wheels of justice can begin to turn. (Indeed many itinerant performers today relish the carefree attitude they can have with parking tickets.) Faced with this mistrust the entertainer, unlike other types of performer, tries hard to show that he or she is harmless and only wishes to provide a pleasing service.

The jongleurs would often combine their performing skills with the sale of merchandise. In many parts of Asia today one can still see 'medicine' shows in which skills are used either to attract a crowd or to demonstrate the powers of certain tonics. This is another link to the shamanistic origins of the entertainer's skills. These travelling entertainers remained on the fringes of society, appearing at markets and fairs, anywhere that a crowd could be found, even public executions. This tradition of street/fairground entertainment continues right up to the present day with the buskers who perform to the cinema queue, or the budgie man in London's Leicester Square (who is reputed to own a Rolls-Royce and send his children to private schools). During their long history, the skills of the street entertainers fed into other areas of performance – for example, the acrobatic skills of the commedia dell'arte – and later on, in the nineteenth century, into the circus and music hall. In the 1920s Brecht was greatly influenced by Karl Valentin, a clown from the variety theatres.

However, the other milieu of the entertainers was in the service of the aristocracy. Some courts in Europe employed a whole range of entertainers; as well as the various types of jester/jongleur there were balladeers, musicians, experts in verbal humour and buffoons. Some of the buffoons acted as if they were crazy, others were actually mentally ill or mentally deficient and served as the butt of much cruel humour. Many of the satirical 'stand-up comics' were highly educated. Some successful entertainers were given land and titles and were received into the aristocracy. From the eighteenth century onwards some aristocrats became conjurors themselves. Astley, who set up the first circus, mainly as a display of horsemanship, was an ex-cavalry officer. This gave the establishment an air of respectability that the fairground entertainers lacked. So popular entertainment was not entirely a product of the fairground.

From the early nineteenth century the growth of cities meant that there was a continuous concentration of population, large enough for the travelling troupes to locate themselves and perform at the increasing number of indoor theatres. These would often combine short melodramatic plays with mimes, singing, dancing, conjuring and all the other traditional skills. The music hall, vaudeville and variety entertainment was a huge industry, catering to the fast-growing urban population, until the arrival of cinema, then television. A popular act would perform two or three times a day, six days a week, fifty weeks in the year. There might be a dozen acts on one bill and several theatres in one city.

As will be seen, many of the performers from this era directly influenced not only the modern buskers but also those working in innovative theatre. First it is necessary to trace the development of the other major influence on modern outdoor performance.

Dada and Performance Art

The strongest influence on European 'experimental theatre' (for lack of a better term) had its origins not in theatre at all, but in the ideas of poets, philosophers and visual artists of continental European capitals during the nineteenth century. The revolutionary political struggles that took place there were a seedbed of new theories as old forms were rejected and new ones tried out. It took generations for new artistic ideas to become accepted but the artists saw their role as fundamental to the transformation of society because they could alter the way people looked at the world. This might be by means of new forms – for example, the impressionists – or through political statement – Delacroix's painting of *Liberty Leading the People*. At the end of the nineteenth century, Alfred Jarry, aided by post-impressionist painters, Bonnard, Vuillard, Toulouse-Lautrec and Serusier, shocked Parisian audiences with his anti-conventional play *Ubu Roi*, which began with the taboo word *merde* – 'shit'. The futurist movement at the beginning of the twentieth century continued the attack on the art traditions and establishment. It also incorporated a revolutionary political stance, identifying with Italian nationalism against Austrian dominance. This ongoing dynamic meant that when the massive social and political upheavals took place during and after the First World War, there was already a current of ideas that produced, on the one hand, the constructivist art in revolutionary Russia, and on the other the nihilist Dada movement in Zurich, in Berlin and later on in Paris and New York.

The Dadaists were primarily visual artists, writers and musicians. One of their aims was to destroy current concepts of art by producing works that were meaningless and were often arrived at by chance rather than design. The first great Dada evening in July 1916 included 'music, the dance, theory, manifestos, poems, pictures, costumes and masks', and a 'phonetic poem' for which a special costume was designed.

My legs were encased in a tight-fitting cylindrical pillar of shiny cardboard which reached to my hips so that I looked like an obelisk. Above this I wore a huge cardboard coat-collar, scarlet inside and gold outside, which was fastened at the neck in such a way that I could flap it like a pair of wings by moving my elbows. I also wore a high, cylindrical blue and white striped witch-doctor's hat.

(Hugo Ball, 1974, *Flight Out of Time*, New York)

This sounds like a costume which would not be out of place in a Dogtroep or IOU show.

Their staged events, both indoors and outdoors, had nothing to do with the conventions that had been built up in the theatrical tradition; they were not intended as theatre but to use performance as a way to provoke the cultured bourgeoisie to the point of riot. The climax of Dada activity in Zurich was the soirée given on 19 April 1919. After a 'simultaneous poem', concluding the first half, had provoked 'shouts, whistles, chanting in unison and laughter', the second half began with a speech cursing the audience.

Then followed music by Hans Heusser, whose tunes or anti-tunes had accompanied Dada since its inauguration at the Cabaret Voltaire. Some slight opposition. A little more greeted Arp's *Wolkenpumpe* ('Cloud Pump'), which was interrupted from time to time, but not often, with laughter and cries of 'Rubbish'. More dances by Perrottet to the music of Schoenberg and then Dr Walter Serner, dressed as if for a wedding in immaculate black coat and striped trousers, with a grey cravat. This tall, elegant figure first carried a headless tailor's dummy on to the stage, then went back to fetch a bouquet of artificial flowers, gave them to the dummy to smell where its head would have been, and laid them at its feet. Finally he brought a chair, and sat astride it in the middle of the platform with his back to the audience. After these elaborate preparations, he began to read from his anarchistic credo, *Letzte Lockerung* ('Final Dissolution'). At last! This was just what the audience had been waiting for.

The tension in the hall became unbearable. At first it was so quiet that you could have heard a pin drop. Then the catcalls began, scornful at first, then furious. 'Rat, bastard, you've got a nerve!' until the noise almost entirely drowned Serner's voice, which could be heard, during a momentary lull, saying the words 'Napoleon was a big strong oaf, after all'.

That really did it. What Napoleon had to do with it, I don't know. He wasn't Swiss. But the young men, most of whom were in the gallery, leaped on to the stage, brandishing pieces of the balustrade (which had survived intact for several hundred years), chased Serner into the wings and out of the building, smashed the tailor's dummy and the chair, stamped on the bouquet. The whole place was in uproar. A reporter from the *Basler Nachrichten*, whom I knew, grasped me by the tie and shouted ten times over, without pausing for breath, 'You're a sensible man normally'. A madness had transformed individual human beings into a mob. The performance was stopped, the lights went up, and faces distorted by rage gradually returned to normal. People were realising that not only Serner's provocations, but also the rage of those provoked, had something inhuman. . . . and that this had been the reason for Serner's performance in the first place.

(From Hans Richter, *Dada – Art and Anti-Art*, pp. 78–9)

The Dadaists promoted a revolutionary viewpoint (although not all of them were left-wing); they were generally anti-authoritarian, anti-art and against capitalism, militarism and nationalism. They were against realism, against rationalism and refuted any attempt at meaning. They refused to codify, regularise, or commercialise their activities and after the move to Paris in 1919 a fragmentation occurred, with some members taking up the banner of the nascent surrealist movement. The element of performance gradually dropped away as the individuals developed their visual work and the initial impact of their events had achieved their effect. During the 1930s and 1940s, a number of them moved across the Atlantic, especially to New York, and further influenced the avant-garde scene there, so that during the 1950s and 1960s a new generation began to experiment in performance with the unique events that became known as 'happenings' (one of which is described on pp. 77–8, in the section on performing artists).

Naturally these developments spread back across the Atlantic,

particularly to Britain, a country previously little affected by the
Dada movement. Here it took root in the postwar boom and
radical early 1960s. Roland Miller started performing in 1964,
Jeff Nuttall and the People Show had their first performance in
1966 and John Fox organised the first performance of Welfare
State in 1968. In 1969 the Bath Arts Workshop, which was a
forerunner of the Natural Theatre Company, was formed by
Phil Shepherd and Ric Knapp. Other pioneers of what became
known in Britain as Performance Art were Neil Hornick and the
Phantom Captain, Ian Hinchcliffe, Rob Conn, Mick Banks and
John Bull Puncture Repair Kit. Later on, in 1974, Forkbeard
Fantasy was formed.

During the 1970s Performance Art developed in a number of
directions. Its earliest exponents were trying to escape the stifl-
ing elitism of the sophisticated spectators and actively seeking a
fresh reaction from an uninitiated public. Another reason they
performed outside art galleries and theatres was because they
were not welcome there; they were forced to perform in the
streets, in basements, old churches or anywhere they could find
because there was nowhere else to do it. Originally most of these
performances were one-offs, unrepeatable, either by design or
because they relied on spontaneity to combust. Eventually
Performance Art achieved a level of acceptance and a large
following. A growing number of the new arts centres supported
and promoted the work and new groups took full advantage of
what became a bandwagon. The return inside, performing
repeatable shows in front of cognoscenti, was a reversal of the
original aims of seeking a fresh public and ultimately led to the
decline of Performance Art, as small audience figures could not
justify the amount of support they began to receive. Those
groups that survived contained elements of the other main
tradition that had been running concurrently to the artistic
developments – that of popular entertainment.

Artist meets entertainer

During the 1970s, in Britain, a synthesis took place. Some artists
acquired a taste for entertainment, others had always had it.
Mark Long of the People Show, amongst others, had a strong
element of the music-hall comic entertainer; with Emil Wolke he
performed acrobatic routines in their *Shredded Wheat Show* in

1980. Their entertaining qualities were shown to the full in the wonderful People Show Cabaret in 1982. Jerome Savary's Grand Magique Circus had a great influence when they visited Britain in the early 1970s. Ken Campbell found a book on tricks and stunts and from that devised his eccentric roadshow.

The process is clearly shown in the development of Forkbeard Fantasy's 'Square Dance'. They started out as performance artists who were keen on contraptions. Four of them took four different colours, one each, and covered themselves from head to foot in them. Then they strapped planks to their feet and attached the ends of the planks to those of their partners so that they formed a square. By co-ordinating their steps they could then rotate. This absurd abstract ritual took on a more figurative quality when, on the occasion of the Queen's Jubilee in 1977, they dressed as bowler-hatted businessmen, painted the planks like the Union Jack and called it 'the Great British Square Dance'. They gave the group of characters an internal conflict of a pecking order, with squabbles over petty one-upmanship. Although the piece was never scripted, a rapport was developed, an awareness of comic timing and playing the dramatic moment. It became more of an absurd Monty Python-type comedy. Forkbeard received criticism from some of the more serious-minded performance artists because, as they readily admit, they are keen to give the audience a good time.

After the hard-edged radicalism of the 1960s there was a softening of artistic, if not political, stance. Popular entertainment and clowning, which had been despised by the performance artists, now became a fashionable pursuit for well-educated performers. Serious, artistic pretensions were debunked by a new generation of performers who were more interested in comedy. This change was accompanied by a shift of artistic activity away from the cities into the countryside. The Barsham and Albion fairs in East Anglia, the Glastonbury Festival and those organised by the Footsbarn associates in south-west England were a fertile meeting ground for artists and entertainers. A new generation of entertainers looked to the work of the performance artists for stimulating ideas. A piece devised by Roland Miller and Shirley Cameron called 'The Cyclamen Cyclists' included a whole group of pink bicycles and pink costumes. This idea was transformed by the Lemmings into a pair of pink policemen with bicycles who became a familiar sight at many of the festivals. These festivals were often quite small so that artists, jugglers, musicians and actors not only saw each other's work but occasionally, as at Hood Fair, near Totnes, in 1978, actually made a joint performance during the course of a long weekend. Unlike their predecessors, many of this new generation had received some form of training in performance. Groups such as Incubus, Kaboodle and Cunning Stunts combined theatre skills with circus skills and live music. The latter were once labelled 'Performance Art Vaudevillians'. The most successful, however, was the Footsbarn Theatre Company. Coming from a training with Jacques Lecoq in Paris, they drew on their local Cornish culture and, like many of these groups, presented both indoor theatre and outdoor popular entertainment, with each aspect of the work affecting the other. A sketch from *A Midsummer Night's Dream* would find its way into their Circus Tosov show, and their theatre work included clowning and direct audience contact drawing on the experience of their outdoor work.

Other influences in Europe

A similar development had occurred in Europe but at a slightly later stage. The tidal wave of war and fascism took longer to recover from and there was the greater cultural and linguistic barrier to the influences from the USA. Gaullist France was actively resistant to trans-Atlantic influences; it was only after the upheavals of 1968 that things started to move.

The most significant historical influence on outdoor theatre in France and Spain was carnival. In a sense carnival and the Feast of Fools prefigured the revolutions of Europe. The same inversion of society and the same anti-authoritarian sentiment were there. When one considers the unquestionable adherence to the church ritual and hierarchy during the Middle Ages, it is incredible to learn the stories of what went on at some of those occasions. Not only were the individual characters in the upper hierarchy ridiculed but the ritual of the mass itself, the most solemn and sacred centre of the whole belief system, was mercilessly parodied – pigs were dressed as bishops, the words of the mass were inverted, and the prelates themselves were sometimes ducked or beaten so much that they had to run for their lives. In a few instances, in France, the military had to be mobilised in order to suppress a minor revolt. The same kind of aggression can be seen in the work of Fuera dels Baus. The village carnival is a very active tradition in northern Spain and other Catalonian groups such as Els Commediants draw on the exhilarating anarchy of carnival as well as its religious imagery. These Catalonian groups have influenced a wave of French groups – Malabar, Generik Vapeur and Archaos. These in turn are having a big impact on the north European outdoor theatre scene.

The one line of development not so far mentioned is that of political theatre and this is because it no longer exerts so much influence on the situation in the early 1990s. The type of agitational propaganda that was used in the Russian Revolution influenced the work of some political theatre groups to come out of the 1960s, such as Red Ladder. Others were influenced by the work of Bread & Puppet and the Living Theater from the USA. As a result of the radicalism at the end of the 1960s, there was a flowering of left-wing political theatre which carried on into the 1970s, with much of it happening on the streets. However, the 1980s saw the demise of many political theatre groups and the virtual disappearance of such activities outdoors. There seem to be several reasons for this. One is the general retreat of socialism, particularly in Britain where the virulently anti-socialist policies of Thatcher transformed the aspirations of the student generation and led many theatre workers to despair at the possibility of social change in their direction. Another reason is that this is no longer an age of confrontational politics; consensus, moderation and negotiation seem to be more the order of the day. Much theatre in eastern Europe is passionately political as newly acquired liberties are taken full advantage of and there is still a residual opposition to all forms of oppression, real or suspected. In the west there is perhaps less to knock against; for young people during the 1980s, global environmental issues became predominant over domestic politics. The experience of Covent Garden Community Theatre, discussed later, demonstrates the effects of these causes. Finally, as discussed later, theatre, even outdoor theatre, is not generally seen as the most effective means of reaching a mass audience.

Many politically motivated performers chose 'community theatre' as a more effective means for social change than changing the system and have been battling away in an adverse political climate. Some of the older generation of groups, such as

Welfare State, still retain their political edge and many of the new French and Spanish groups have a kind of punk anarchist/ socialist radicalism about them. There are still plenty of outdoor theatre performers with something to say (discussed more fully in the chapter on communicators, pp. 67–73) but, because of the difficulty of hearing text outdoors, complex issues are nowadays more generally dealt with by those working in indoor theatre.

Finally it has to be said that there are a host of other influences on the contemporary scene that have nothing to do with performance history. The Mad Max films have influenced several French groups. Robotic break-dancing is derived from a Decroux mime technique but has more to do with the music/rap scene. In this age of individualism styles vary enormously but are greatly affected by what designs the performers have on the audience and this is the subject to be considered next.

Part I

The driving force

MOTIVATIONS

Why do people feel compelled to do theatre in unconducive situations like streets and parks? Anyone who has tried it will know that the first time out there can be a very nerve-racking experience even for experienced actors, it is a very exposed situation and requires quite a courageous leap. Most performers find it quite hard to articulate why they got into it in the first place.

If you ask buskers why they are working in this way the first thing they will say is because of the money. Even though money is often a main motivation, performers cannot live by bread alone. They must receive some pleasure in what they are doing, otherwise the performance will quickly become mechanical and dispirited; when that happens they will not earn much because it is the fullness of spirit that audiences appreciate and are willing to dig deep in their pockets for. It is a very pleasing way to earn money because you receive it as a gift and can feel satisfied that it is a fair measure of the amount of enjoyment you have given. (There are of course techniques to maximise this 'measure of appreciation' but these will be discussed later.) What is more, the amounts received can be fairly substantial and if the situation is right the performer can then be tempted to churn out as many shows as possible in one day, earning hundreds of pounds in some cases. However, this option is rarely available and in any case would quickly become impossible in terms of energy and enjoyment, resulting in diminishing returns.

Other stated reasons might be the freedom from routine, the spontaneity, the ability to travel and the fact that it is a very good way to meet people because they get to know you (and presumably like you) by means of the show. Also it provides a good training ground since the moments when the show succeeds or drops are clearly shown in the swelling or diminishing of the crowd. Sometimes performers will add that it is a good way to be seen in order to get other work and that at least it is better to be active than passively unemployed.

There is one other factor that is rarely mentioned but is certainly present particularly with successful solo performers and that is the element of megalomania. Anyone who has seen much street theatre must be familiar with the technique of working up a crowd: the performer repeats a cue for cheering and clapping, and cajoles and encourages each time until the desired effect is achieved. Later on in the show the performer may suddenly cue the audience again, switching on and off the applause. At its best a simple flick of the finger can immediately animate hundreds of people. This is only one of the many ways of controlling an audience. The audience gives the performer power to take liberties; he or she can be rude and outrageous and still get away with it, complete strangers can be made to do things they would never do normally and people in uniform can be outfaced. The street performer relishes this sense of power in much the same way as the rock star or political demagogue. The effects of this power will be discussed at the end of the book; for the moment it is enough to recognise the importance of this chemistry between performer and audience.

All performers want to make an impression on the audience so that they leave the spectators with something to think about, smile about, or be outraged about. However, once the work starts to be organised in terms of scheduled performances, fees and contracts, a more businesslike approach is adopted and the craft becomes more self-conscious. The performers may want to make a statement, to comment or satirise. They may also want to enlarge people's concept of theatre or reach audiences who do not normally go to the theatre. They may enjoy playing in different unusual environments and finally they may just enjoy making beautiful images and presenting them.

People are complicated and artists more complicated than most, but for the purposes of the book it seems useful to categorise performers according to their motives. Most performers have many different motives and it is difficult to find examples that are purely of one type, but most would be able to identify themselves with one group more than others. It is a question more of emphasis than of neat pigeon-holing. The first category, entertainers, is the most obvious. Animators, provocateurs, communicators and performing artists are discussed in the chapters that follow on.

Chapter 3

Entertainers

For the purposes of this book entertainers are defined as those with the simple aim of pleasing the audience, either by making them laugh or by impressing them with skills such as juggling, acrobatics, or magic. Very little is demanded of the public in terms of participation or thought. In this sense it is virtually identical to busking done by musicians, operating on the principle that the more pleasure is received by the public the more money is made. It is probably the most numerous type of performer and the one most commonly identified with street performing.

Apart from the financial considerations there are other benefits to be received from entertaining people. The most obvious one is that of giving pleasure to a large number of people. Most entertainers try to appeal to as wide a range of audience as possible and, outdoors, the performer is much more accessible to the public. This means that they will receive not only direct praise from young and old, but thanks and affection too. It is not uncommon for good outdoor entertainers to receive unsolicited appreciative letters from older people and drawings from children, who seem to form an instant bonding with clown characters (they express this by the curious method of running up and hitting them). Simply aiming to please is not a high ambition but it lacks the pretensions of other types of performer. It is a joy to create laughter; applause can always be induced and is not necessarily a true response from the audience. Laughter, on the other hand, as a spontaneous expression by the audience, cannot be faked.

Many entertainers who use circus skills also get pleasure from impressing the public. Most mature ones will be aware of the limitation of their skills; they will have seen people better themselves so, however much the audience may be impressed, they are aware that skills, like virtues, are only comparative. However, there is, of course, a certain swelling of pride to be had in knowing that, even if you are not the best juggler in the country, at least you are the best in that town on that day. It is the audience that gives performers status, and the respect given will obviously vary from place to place. Jugglers are two a penny in some places and treated with great respect in others. Buskers will travel far to go to towns where their act is unusual. Ten or fifteen years ago buskers were nearly all musicians and at that time it was relatively easy to make a success out of a little magic, juggling and stunt show because it was unusual. Nowadays new variations have to be found.

[The function of the entertainer is to be light and joyful, to add colour and activity. As such, entertainers are often used to 'decorate' another activity, to keep people amused while they are doing or waiting for something else] For example, the jongleur troupes of the Middle Ages were invited into the banqueting halls of the aristocracy to provide a bit of distraction while the eating went on, a sort of low-tech TV dinner. Today entertainers are often encouraged by tourist boards to make a lively 'decoration' to re-pedestrianised shopping precincts in order to enhance the historical feel of tourist towns or they are used to add a bit of colour to dull, modern shopping precincts.

Because entertainers try to be acceptable to the widest possible tastes, they tend to be fairly deferential to the status quo and confirm widely held assumptions and beliefs. Their style is often quite traditional, although this does not exclude original new versions of old acts. By keeping an uncontroversial profile they are able to survive periods of political oppression. This is not to say that they do not embrace modern methods but, like Chaplin (resisting 'talkies' to the last), they resist them until they are overtaken and replaced.

The humble tradition of harmless entertainment may be looked down upon by some but it is important to acknowledge that the passing on of skills over the centuries provided a rich source that fuelled the commedia dell'arte during the Renaissance and fed into circus, music hall, vaudeville and variety during the eighteenth and nineteenth centuries. With the decline of these forms in the late twentieth century, it is the

street performers who helped to keep the tradition going, leading to the current interest in 'New' Circus, 'New' Variety and
even 'New' Mime. The end of pigeon-holing of art forms and
the consequent mixing of disciplines is a welcome development;
the inherited skills of the entertainers are once again beginning
to feed back into contemporary theatre.

BOÎTE À PANDORE: A CLASSIC STREET ACT

Boîte à Pandore (Pandora's Box) is a Quebecois duo performing
mainly in France, who have developed their act from a ten-
minute busking show up to a thirty-five-minute show that is
booked on a fee-paying basis. It is an example of how constant
repetition and continual readjustment over many years can
transform a simple skills show into a sophisticated entertainment. It has a charming and easy confidence born out of many
years' practice.

The set-up is a lesson in practical efficiency. Although there is
equipment for slack rope, juggling, percussion, unicycle, a chair,
costumes and props, it is all carried on two carts, small enough to
get in and out of their ancient camper van and with sturdy
wheels to go over cobbles and kerbs. All the equipment and
costumes are united by a colour design of black and yellow. The
duo's name is prominently displayed on the lid of an open trunk
– an important feature when the show won't be advertised in any
other way.

One of the ways to build a crowd is by setting up equipment in
an interesting way so that it actually becomes a part of the
performance. They make a clear statement that something is
about to happen by prising up cobbles and banging in stakes,
expertly judging whether there are pipes or cables underground. The stakes anchor the slack rope and there is much
experimenting with the tension which begins to draw in the
public. A rope which is then laid on the ground defines the
shape and distance of the front row. While the rest of the
equipment is being set up and the costumes put on, there is an
easy banter with the public about the weather or the situation;
organising the position of the crowd provides opportunities for
playful direct contact. All is unhurried and unforced, indeed
there is a waiting time for the appointed hour when nothing
much happens but which has the effect of building tension and

expectation. As a final part of the set-up the man puts on his last piece of costume – his hat; this involves flipping it up from his foot on to his head and there is much play had with the problem of the wind (real or imaginary). The whole set-up from first stepping out of the van until this moment has taken about twenty minutes.

The problem with skills is how to make them dramatically interesting – a pure display of skill is not enough and jugglers who have excellent skill can be quite tedious. One way Pandore solve this is by the clear relationship between the two of them. The man is the clown and the woman the boss. There are also the relationships with the audience, with the volunteers and with their dog, 'Monsieur'. Another way to make it more dramatically interesting is by building up tension, using these relationships, and then releasing it with comedy. Variety is the other ingredient; for example, since they do several juggling routines they have to spread them throughout the show. They are constantly revising the order of acts bearing in mind several factors; contact with the audience needs to be established as early as possible and so participation tends to be concentrated in the first half, with the more spectacular skills towards the end. The slack rope act is the high point three-quarters of the way through and is followed by a couple of acts that can be done by one partner so that the other can go round with the hat, if this is appropriate to the situation. After the finale there are a couple of endearing magic tricks that leave the audience with the feeling of being given that little bit extra.

The show starts with some basic club juggling with percussion accompaniment. If the man drops a club the 'boss' orders him to do press-ups as punishment – this sets up a running gag and establishes their relationship straightaway. A volunteer is then selected to throw in one club to the juggling pattern and then throw in two. If anything goes wrong they both have to do press-ups. This section is finished by juggling fire clubs with the audience clapping in time, to a beat set by the drums. This is followed by the first act with 'Monsieur': they sing and play 'How Much Is that Doggy in the Window' and the dog barks on cue, or at least is supposed to, but either way the laughs come. Then back to juggling, this time with clubs passing between the two of them; he has a harmonica and she has a whistle for the necessary musical accompaniment. They do a nice snatching routine with

Figure 2 Boîte à Pandore give a 'free juggling lesson'

three clubs, while swapping hats, and then go on to six clubs, playing the drama of picking up the club that has dropped – building the tension by not having the time to grab it, and then releasing it by kicking the club over to the partner and giving them the problem. More audience play follows as they get someone else to stand between them as they pass clubs front and back, the main drama being on the face of the volunteer.

The tension is built for the slack rope act by pretending not to know how to do it. Every possible gag is used; the poles come apart, getting up on to it presents comic problems, the man gets his finger stuck in one pole, spikes himself sitting on the other pole, walks his feet across but leaves his hands on the poles, plays being scared and wobbles on the rope. Eventually he succeeds and finishes by juggling, passing clubs from up there. The unicycle act follows the same pattern; it is not the success that is important so much as all the problems encountered on the way – he gives 'a free unicycle lesson' (to show how hard it is) and, when he does get on, he plays the danger of nearly falling off into the front row. This again finishes with the main skill; this time bouncing up and down skipping a rope.

After these big acts it is good to focus in on something much smaller – juggling ping-pong balls from the mouth. He plays victim and pulls funny faces as she orders him to put more balls in his mouth. This is followed by the second dog act in which Monsieur refuses to jump through a hoop but happily jumps through hooped arms, legs and then over a headstand with split legs. (This ends with the dog leaping in the air, skipping a rope and a final pyramid with all three of them.) The last act is the most skilful – juggling five balls on the ground with everybody clapping. This would be the time to pass the hat. After the end-of-show announcements there is an encore of a card trick and quick clown routine with a chair.

The whole operation is *'efficace'* – combining effectiveness with efficiency. There is no self-indulgent time-spinning, no excess of props or costumes, it is lightweight (in both senses of the word) but very well crafted for maximum effect with minimum effort.

METAFOLIS: UNTRADITIONAL ENTERTAINERS

Not all entertainers conform to the normal pattern; Metafolis are unusual in that they have a story. It is quite highly stylised both in terms of acting and format and has a modern untraditional feel. They are a trio – two Frenchmen and a German who perform a play based on the type of comic strip books known as *bande dessinée* in France. One of them plays the artist sketching out the story which is acted out by the other two. In reality he operates the electronic sound effects and adds vocal effects with a microphone. This format enables them to play tricks like freezing the action (while the artist has his lunch) and rewinding the story as the artist uses a huge eraser to rub out what he had created. They also change the location of the story by suddenly switching the soundtrack of a Victorian London pub to jungle sounds. This gives the whole show a wonderful sense of surprise and surrealism.

Like many of the *bande dessinée* books the element of grotesque creeps in – the second half of the show involves an American cowboy and his daughter being nice to each other until the cowboy accidentally pushes her too hard on the swing and she flies off and is killed. The same actions are then repeated but this time in grotesque form: the dutiful daughter becomes wickedly naughty, putting salt in her father's coffee instead of sugar and doing a black magic ritual on an effigy of him, pulling its legs so they extend; and sure enough the cowboy returns on massive legs (dressed stilts) which are then attached to a construction in the set and he is rotated by his giggling daughter.

This is certainly not a traditional sort of show; there is a lot of swearing which runs counter to the mainstream entertainers' desire to be inoffensive. The material owes almost nothing to tradition and is highly original in its style, format and sense of black humour. The set consists of a backdrop of corrugated iron in a curved wall. (This is very effective at throwing the voice forward and reflecting the flaming torches.) The stunt with the rotating stilts is inventive and unique, not presented as a trick but cleverly integrated into the story. The world they create is, if anything, reminiscent of the absurdity of Monty Python's Flying Circus, which also played tricks with sequence and repetition. However, they reveal their origins with two displays of juggling; at heart they are simply good entertainers. They don't seek to challenge the audience or communicate a message and there is no audience participation. Their experience of street performing can be seen in the quality of their acting. It is relaxed in the sense of not being afraid of the situation, very precise in timing and gesture but capable of intense, 110 per cent full-on extremes of gesture and expression.

Chapter 4

Animators

Most outdoor shows have some form of audience participation, either by having a volunteer 'onstage' or by getting the audience to respond vocally in some way. However, there are a small number of groups and solos who use audience interaction not just for part of the show but as the main act itself. The aim of these animators is to play a game with the audience. They may do this 'onstage' with individuals or with up to six or seven volunteers play-acting under instruction. The other way to do it is to involve the entire audience in the game, which is what usually happens when they are led on a journey. In both cases they enter into the contract of 'Let's pretend'. The animators may be part of the action, as is usually the case on journeys, or they may simply direct the action.

One of the more established performers at the Pompidou Centre in Paris is Jean Gheuse. Over the years he has cultivated quite a following, so that when he arrives at his usual performing area, the waiting crowd gives him a round of applause much like a famous conductor being welcomed on to the stage. Indeed he even has a little stick with which he cues and encourages the willing public. He gets the audience to act out stories of romance, building up the number of characters one by one as the plot develops. He gives actions and text to suit each individual, repeated, if necessary, to develop and extend the situation. This type of performance is obviously quite risky in the sense that there is no actual show and it relies on the ability of the animator to improvise with non-professionals. There is often a simple scenario but by itself it wouldn't add up to much; the success of the piece depends entirely on the skill of the performer in choosing and animating the members of the public.

Another tried and tested method of animating is the one pioneered by such groups as Doggs Troupe in the 1970s. Characters arrive at the scheduled place and time of the show. They have a problem; they might be explorers without a map, detectives looking for clues, or local people who suspect the planners are preparing to build a motorway through their park. In any case they explain the problem to the audience and ask them what they should do. While suggestions are being made, another character arrives with new information and suggests they all go to a new location to find out more. When they arrive an incident happens, a fight with someone running away or a character that needs help. Gradually the information begins to form a whole picture of the situation with the audience fitting all the pieces of the puzzle together. Finally there is a confrontation or a solution that resolves the story and the audience is thanked for its co-operation.

This method was used by many community theatre groups as means to empower the audience to find out information and to take action themselves rather than being passive spectators. Children certainly become very excited by the 'Treasure Hunt' aspect and often seem totally to disregard the knowledge that it is really only a play. Their imagination is stimulated as they try to find out answers to the mystery that is being unfolded. They are encouraged to feel that the choices they make will affect the course of the play. It does not have to involve a journey to different locations, the characters can just arrive at the same spot, but normally there is one. This allows for some pre-arranged surprises. The journey created by Red Earth, which is described later (pp. 148–52), has an element of this method. One of the problems of this format is that it is hard to involve large numbers of people and in any case crowd control can be difficult, with excited children running off in all directions to look for clues. It has been known for the villain of the piece to be discovered, in costume but 'off duty', by children who then forcefully apprehend him and thus disrupt the next part of the plot.

This type of scenario is not dissimilar to theatrical events in Bali. At the final episode of a three-day village festival, which I was fortunate to be present at, the white-masked witch god, Rangda, emerged from her part of the temple and slowly made her way towards the performing area where three masked, comic soldiers had been defiantly swaggering and boasting of their courage. Rangda began to make lunges towards them and the rest of the spectators, who recoiled in genuine fear. (In the Hindu tradition a representation of a god is actually imbued with power.) These lunges became larger until the circle began to break up, running in all directions so that the whole village became involved in a chaotic running battle as the brave tried to goad Rangda back into her part of the temple.

Audiences vary and there will obviously be some that are hard to have much fun with. Most animators tend to stick to one location in order to cut down on variable factors. The make-up of an audience (and therefore how they respond) will vary from hour to hour in the same location – a lunchtime crowd has more time to stop than one at mid-morning. Cultural differences are even more surprising. In the traditional Nigerian format the emphasis is on experiencing the dances rather than spectating. Similarly the story-tellers are used to an audience that will comment, criticise and assist vocally without any prompting. Audiences there are also used to providing a basic rhythm, either clapped or sung, over which the story-teller sings/recites the story-line. European audiences would find this difficult as they are used to a more formal, 'polite' attention focused on the performer. The responsibility for the success of the event in the African situation lies with the whole participating community. In the European situation the more sophisticated is the public, the more this responsibility is pushed on to the performer. Highbrow theatre audiences in London or Paris are not the easiest to animate.

The role of the animator is as important today as it has been in the past. The function of traditional African dance is to change the consciousness of the dancers. It does this, first, by bringing the attention of the dancers into their bodies through the enjoyment of movement. Secondly, there is a diminishing of the ego by merging into the same rhythm as a large group. This loss of individualism is deliberately encouraged in modern armies through the method of parade-ground drill. Drill, however, lacks the third element of the African dance, which is the release. Anyone who has danced vigorously will know that the combination of relaxation and force, supported by the right rhythms, generates its own energy permitting one to dance longer than if the same energy were put into forceful work movements or the movements of old-fashioned 'military' physical exercise. Aerobics and modern dance, from reggae to acid house, are sustainable because of this principle. The dancer can dance for hours and at the end will feel the cathartic release that has been lost in nearly all western theatre.

Dele Charley from Sierra Leone explained his method of political theatre under censorship. It is not by bluntly attacking the government but by animating the community to dance and share their joy, grief, hopes and frustrations, giving them a positive sense of solidarity and power by experiencing the sharing of their emotions. In a sense the body is cleansed of the emotions, danced out by the total expression of them. This primary function of art touches upon primary religious manifestations. In primitive societies the animator is the shaman, working up the dancers to a state of trance. The shaman is responsible for the 'release' of self-destructive forces (demons) from the body. Nowadays the 'charismatic' preachers use singing, dancing and the call-and-answer technique to work the congregation out of their everyday consciousness. The street theatre animator is also able to break through the shell of everyday existence by getting people to do what they would never do without assistance, that is, to make fools of themselves in front of a large group of strangers and be thanked and appreciated by that group. Their self-image is enhanced and they have left behind that judgemental part of themselves that says that we have to be clever to perform. A good animator will make it quite clear that it is not a question of obeying the given instructions correctly but of reinterpreting them in your own way. In other words to do what comes naturally; to be fully yourself.

The whole business of carnival is about letting go of normal modes of behaviour and this is partly achieved by endless bouts of drinking, dancing and singing. The other way to shake people out of their normal patterns is with the element of danger. The sheer quantity of fireworks and their proximity is an outstanding feature of the Catalonian carnivals. Some groups from there, such as Bat, animate the crowd by running amongst them, showering them with sparks from fireworks of the Roman candle type and deafening them with close explosions. Unless one is prepared and alert, hair and clothing get burnt. Some young people relish the sparks; covering their heads, they dance

Figure 3 Bat – Spanish pyrotechnic theatre at
Tarrega, 1989

in a rain of fire. Bat also use a number of other devices to scatter
the crowd: bicycles pouring out sparks and a number of pre-set
pyrotechnics that are ignited once the spectators have been led
down a particular route, into close proximity. When Bat organised the finale of the Tarrega Festival in 1989, the centre of
activity led the crowd around the town, the scale of the pyrotechnics getting larger all the time. All sorts of fire-emitting images
were used, dragons and devils chased spectators up and down,
crushed into the narrow streets until they arrived just outside
the town where the main display went up. Els Commediants
used similar methods at a notorious performance at Battersea
Park in London (see pp. 49–51). The Paris-based Opposito is
another company who use fireworks to keep the spectators on

their toes and to provide a central focus to their journey around the town. All forms of journey can be seen as a type of animation, because the spectators put themselves into the hands of the animators and are physically led through an experience. They are much more vulnerable than they would be in a stationary performance, although the level of expected participation can vary considerably.

The society we live in advocates the freedom of the individual. As with all freedoms there is a negative corollary; increased individuality leads to increased isolation. In this context the role of the animator in opening people up to one another and to themselves, in a spirit of shared play, serves an ever-important function.

BETO AND THE TECHNIQUES OF THE ANIMATOR

Beto is a Spanish clown who has developed his participation act on the streets of Barcelona. He has acquired great expertise in choosing and handling his audience. He creates a warm atmosphere in which chosen members of the public can play without feeling embarrassed. This is a great skill. He performs entirely without words using gentle mime techniques and vocal sound to imitate and communicate. His gentleness is in stark contrast to the aggressiveness of some British and French performers but is an absolutely essential ingredient for this type of act.

As soon as he is ready to start he begins to draw attention to himself by imitating the looks and movements of people passing by. He carries simple props such as a pair of glasses, a plastic ice-cream cone and a scarf ready to pull out of his pockets if the moment is right. These are gentle, playful imitations that can go into simple improvisation if the person is up to it. Gradually a crowd gathers and Beto draws the centre of attention towards the sound system and props that he has prepared at the chosen site. Then he arranges the shape of the crowd, enlarging the space so that the front row is established, and then increases its size by getting them to applaud. He builds into this by using a call-and-answer method; he claps once, they must clap once, then he claps twice so they repeat it, finally he claps fast and then they applaud. This is developed into them cheering and applauding his 'entrance', which is in fact just walking to the front centre of the space in a very grand manner. This is

Figure 4 Beto making initial contact with individuals

repeated several times as he gently cajoles those individuals not getting into it, making fun of their indifference, shyness, or self-importance. He literally is 'making fun' so that those who receive the attention of the whole crowd in this way start to laugh along with the joke and relax into the atmosphere.

At this stage Beto is beginning to take stock of the members of the audience, noticing those with fun possibilities – fatness, baldness, beards, unusual clothes, a distinctive laugh – and particularly those who are not self-conscious. He may not appear to notice them in the early part of the show but when the time is right he will know exactly whom to go to. Some performers will develop a relationship with one sympathetic member of the audience but Beto is continually throwing the event open to include as many different sorts of people as possible. He will also enlarge the space further by making contact with people watching from windows on the other side of the street. I imagine these tactics must increase the amount of money thrown into the hat at the end because he is contacting the older, higher-status people as well as the more obviously playful, but poorer, young. Having attracted more audience with the sounds of clapping and cheering, he starts the first sequence. He produces a tiny toy microphone and switches on his tape-recorder playing a sound-track of a bouncy jig with pauses that are filled with a variety of odd sound effects. He gets the audience to clap along to the tune and then, at the pause, he holds the microphone to his chest and the sound of a heartbeat is heard, then the tune recommences (with the clapping) and at the next pause he goes to someone else's heart, this time the sound heard is a very fast heartbeat, or the sound of a bell tolling or glass breaking. He chooses an appropriate person each time so that, for example, a romantic-looking teenager has the sound of birds gaily singing in her heart; someone who looks rather glum has no sound at all and is pronounced dead. He has different techniques of approaching people, sometimes moving obliquely towards them without look-ing and then, as the sound effect comes on, suddenly turning round. Other times he makes eye contact from the other side of the space and approaches them slowly and obviously. Although this sequence sounds silly and insubstantial its purpose is only to warm up the audience for what is to follow. It works well because it doesn't require those chosen to do anything but stand there. They don't have to come out of the crowd and the alternation of pauses with the light melody lightens the atmos-phere after each encounter. The rhythm of the alternation relaxes them because they know they will only be the focus of attention for a very short time.

Once this warm-up is completed he moves on to the main action, which is to get a man and a woman from the audience to enact a simple love scene and a second man to challenge the first; they fight, one is killed and the lovers reunite – a time-honoured scenario. The skill is in choosing the right people and getting them to play. He avoids people who may themselves be performers, not so much out of a fear of being upstaged but rather to get the fresh amateur approach that can be much funnier than someone doing all the actions correctly. He always ensures that the participants make their own decision to come out of the crowd. Although he may playfully threaten them with a toy club or gun, he never either drags them out of the audience or pleads with them – both are acts of desperation and the marks of a bad animator. Obviously once they have decided to step into the space the audience is cued for applause. This is followed by getting them to do simple little steps or arm gestures. Each time Beto will demonstrate and then hand over to the volunteer. Gradually these movements are enlarged so that they actually are being led through a physical warm-up without realising it – jumping up and down and waving their arms in big circles. Then they are costumed with, for example, a hat, a scarf, or a plastic nose and glasses. This costuming is important because it allows them to become different from their normal selves, just in the way that putting on a mask can free the individual from his or her 'self'. So one by one they are brought out and played with; Beto uses increasingly high energy, difficult-to-follow movements and clever mime technique to demonstrate what they must do at every stage; they try to repeat it. The comedy comes out of their interpretation of the moves not by their being correct. Gradually they gain confidence to try their own actions and to break through their inhibitions – lying on the ground, kissing total strangers and losing themselves in the role. Carefully handled like this, the audience witnesses the liberation of these three people from their inhibitions so that the final bow is warm; joyous and truly celebratory. In this way Beto is like the shaman freeing them from their devils using the supportive power of the whole group.

One of the perils of street performers is the insensitivity of other performers. On one of the occasions that I saw Beto, he spent twenty minutes building up the atmosphere, getting his three protagonists into their actions, and was probably five minutes from the end of the show, with the subsequent collection, when a group of drummers and stilt-walkers came dancing down the narrow street, forcing Beto's crowd to scatter from the fireworks that were being thrown. He waited for them to go past to see if he could recover the carefully created atmosphere but the passage took too long and so he stoically accepted the destruction of his show and the loss of his revenue.

LA COMPAGNIE EXTRÊMEMENT PRÉTENTIEUSE

La Compagnie Extrêmement Prétentieuse is a company of three people with a strong Lecoq basis for their work. Apart from their street work they also perform and organise a 'dîner-spectacle' in which the audience is formally served a multi-course meal by bizarre comic waiters and a series of surprising and surreal events accompany each stage in the proceedings. They also perform an intense, precise indoor theatre show influenced by the bouffon style.

Their street work also involves waiters. It is specifically designed for the terraces of outdoor restaurants which are common in continental Europe. The pretext is that they are looking for work and aim to prove their worthiness to the unsuspecting patron and his clientele. Their extravagant and elaborate methods of doing whatever is required eventually go wrong and they have to make a spectacular and hasty retreat from the disaster they have caused.

The tactic of offering a service is extremely effective; everyone likes to have things done for them so who can refuse, especially when the chosen clients are already installed in their places. The danger is the risk of forcing too much attention on people who just want to have a quiet drink but the beauty of the situation is that the chosen 'volunteers' don't have to do anything and that even a refusal adds to the hopelessness of the eager-to-please waiters. They manage to maintain a very fine balance between pushing a situation to its limits – for example, by rearranging the whole of the rest of the café to suit the whim of their willing victims – and avoiding the real displeasure of the patron and the rest of the customers. In practice there is usually no problem – the patron and customers love the fun as long as they feel reassured that the anarchy is somehow under control. However, accidents are bound to happen in this situation; drinks can be spilled or worse, as in one show that I saw – they were in the act of getting an absurdly high angle for a snapshot of the happy clients, when the table-top on which they were standing broke and there was a beautiful moment when all eyes turned to the beefy manager to see the real reaction to the real dramatic situation. The incident passed without interruption, although his steely smile became a little cooler. To protect themselves and to avoid unnecessary stress to all concerned they ask the organisers to take out insurance against all possible types of mishap; it must be quite a uniquely worded policy.

Their skill lies in the sensitivity to the situation and the seamless combination of routines and improvisation. The situation is obviously ripe for possibilities – the customers are being asked to demand whatever they desire and they may make impossible demands that will have to be dealt with somehow. However, the company has such quickness of wit and imagination that there is no danger of their being flummoxed. The improvisation is backed up by routines which get them into and out of tricky situations – for example, the simple act of lighting a cigarette involves the head of Monsieur Pilatte being placed near the customer. On top of his head is taped the striking side of a box of matches. Mademoiselle Leonie clears a passage through the crowd for Monsieur Gordon who dramatically makes long elegant strides towards the table, then swipes the upheld match across Monsieur Pilatte's cranium, straight to the awaiting cigarette, which usually isn't ready because the customer is laughing so much. Monsieur Pilatte has a vast array of implements in pockets on the inside of his waistcoat ready for every eventuality – every sort of cutlery, of course, but also spanners, scissors, surgical appliances, sticky tape and round his backside under his long white apron a waste disposal pedal bin. The proceedings are usually terminated by smoke issuing from this bin and the ensuing panic as Gordon and Leonie throw drinks at him in order to put him out.

One of the problems they encounter is that the environment must be much the same each time. If there are no cafés then they must play the game of looking for one. This has fewer possibilities. If it is cold and rainy then they can go inside a café but it is difficult to bring a large audience in with them. Within the pretext of their characters and situation they are not able to ensure good sight-lines and choosing a suitable table to focus in on can be quite alarming for customers who are quietly having a drink as hundreds of people swarm around them. Forcing theatre on to people who do not want it directly contradicts the main aim of street theatre – it alienates rather than bringing people together. Another problem is how to finish; there is no curtain to hide behind once it is over and they strictly observe the first rule of walkabout – never drop character in public. In one situation I saw at the festival in Aurillac, they were unable to

Figure 5 La Compagnie Extrêmement Prétentieuse offer a service

shake off the audience after they had made their exit from the café and so they were pursued by scores of people through a park. Leonie tried to 'disappear' by blending in with figures in a war memorial (Figure 17, p. 174), Gordon was shouted at by the park-keeper for walking on the grass so he promptly sat on the remains of the broken table removing the offending feet from the afore-said herbage. There seemed no escape from the spectators, who continued to follow as the trio observed rule two – if there is an audience keep performing. Eventually they suddenly leapt on to a passing bus just as the doors were closing and were whisked away to some distant suburb, from where they had to walk back because, of course, they had no money in their costumes.

The first time I ever did walkabout I had no idea what to do so in desperation I borrowed a plastic flower and offered it to people to smell. Although ridiculously simple and stupid, this tactic did have the right effect – through the object I offered myself to play while giving them the possibility of an exit from the situation by refusing. The Compagnie Extrêmement Prétentieuse have developed this simple offering of a service into a highly sophisticated and vital art form.

ELS COMMEDIANTS GIVE THEM HELL

Els Commediants are a Catalonian group, who have found a way to animate spectators by means of fireworks and physical abuse. In the particular show that is described here, they use the journey format and it shows how they manage to move large crowds as well as having a profound effect on them. Everyone who saw this renowned show (which I was unfortunately unable to be present at) has a different story to tell but I am grateful to Robin Morley for the following description.

The show was put on as part of the London International Festival of Theatre in 1985. It was free and had received extensive publicity, including articles in colour supple-ments, so a large crowd, of perhaps four or five thousand, congregated around the ornamental lake in Battersea Park. It was supposed to start at about nine o'clock and we waited till half past nine, quarter to ten, and it gradually got darker. It became quite obvious that there was a prob-lem. What had happened was that a whole scene was supposed to have taken place on the lake but for some reason they couldn't get any of the engines in the boats working. So something happened on the lake over by the ornamental rocks and then nothing else happened after that. There was quite a lot of frustration building up. Then performers started to appear in trees and on tops of buildings with fireworks and wearing colourful costumes and leather devil masks. A band appeared making a fantastic row, chaotic music and really loud; they were marching up and down and slowly this began to build into a whole movement of people. They started to throw fireworks down at the feet of the audience – these were not little jumping jacks but serious Spanish fireworks – and they were doing it very skilfully, it was dangerous but not stupid. With these, there were other pyrotechnics and lots of smoke so you began finding you weren't able to see everywhere and, of course, it was starting to get dark. Various floodlights came up.

There was not just one but several bands marching up and down through the crowd and people got the idea they were going somewhere and they moved off through a little fence and down an avenue of trees. Because fireworks were being thrown down at people's feet a whole crowd of people would rush off. It is a sensation that Fuera dels Baus create, where the whole crowd moves as a body and you move because everyone moves. You cannot see why or where you are moving and this creates a really powerful energy. We were walking down this avenue of trees and suddenly all these fireworks went off above people's heads, bangers falling and sparks everywhere so, again, the level of excitement went up. Some people thought it was wonderful, others hated it, many people later found they had holes burnt in their coats. In other places there were lines of fire across the path that we had to cross over.

Eventually we ended up in a big open space with scaffolding towers. There were devils up in the towers and they started to pelt the crowd with bags of flour, these hit people and the flour went everywhere. They also threw cabbages and lettuces so you were being physically abused and assaulted. Then the crowd moved off again with the bands still marching up and down making a cacophony of music. People started to look different now, some had come in quite smart clothes which were covered in flour and cabbage. We came to another area which had a tower building in it where there was a set-piece performance with a dragon. Finally we came to an empty lido where there were figures in white on the ornamental fountains; there we watched the triumph of good over evil – a very spectacular firework show.

Els Commediants, like Archaos and Royal de Luxe, are very uncompromising; they will not go anywhere unless they can do what they want to do. For this show they had to work with a GLC fire officer and their policy was to show him only a limited amount of what was about to happen so, for example, he was not aware of the fireworks let off above the crowd. It was even said that the Special Branch arrived and confiscated whole boxes of fireworks because they had been smuggled into the country. Because of all this they have not been allowed back to London, nor have they had much inclination to come.

Chapter 5

Provocateurs

Entertainers are deferential to the status quo – they just want to do their job and please people. Animators want to break down the barriers between people and get them to loosen up individually. There are other performers, however, who are more concerned with loosening up society as a whole. They are not concerned with simply amusing the public and may actually disdain such an empty exercise. They may play with the audience but it is a game with the audience's fears and expectations. They ask questions of society by going to the limits of conventionally acceptable behaviour. By occasionally stepping over the mark they confront the spectators with their own taboos. On a personal level they may hold specific moral or political positions but they choose not to preach a message, rather these provocateurs stick their tongues out at society, poking fun at it and challenging its comfortable beliefs, much like images from religious art in which small devils torment saints with their horrid little forks.

It has often been said that the devilish side of things holds much more fascination than the pure of heart. Dante's and Milton's works are evidence of that. The 'baddie' roles are also more fun to perform because they release that side of us that we normally keep suppressed. Acknowledgement of that darker side of humanity often reveals a truth that is uncomfortable for those who want to see and hear no evil. The classic example of this in European history is the total inversion of society during carnival and the Feast of Fools. However, no deliberate and credible challenge to the feudal system was being advocated, simply a revolt against its strict regulations. It is a refreshing thought that whenever in history humanity becomes too constricted, as under totalitarian regimes, it will eventually find ways of expressing its desires. Too much pressure in a contained system requires a release valve. In this sense the provocateurs play a very important function in society. They represent the individual's complaint against the way the system operates. Circus clown acts in India have clown priests and landowners, in pre-glasnost Russia the military and police were targets, in Kenya I saw the parody of village elders and shaman in a comic circumcision ritual.

Although they provoke and challenge they do not take it upon themselves to provide answers. They don't advocate a different system but, by focusing on common complaints, bring everyone to feel that the truth of what they are saying has to be recognised. This licensed foolery is similar to the traditional role of the court jester – tolerated and valued because they can see through the artifice and manipulation of the court and speak the truth. At carnival time in Switzerland the local 'character' is traditionally allowed this same licence and may pop out at any time, anywhere, sticking out his tongue, being generally outrageous and saying out loud all those whispered bits of village gossip, pointing out the pretensions and making a comic nuisance of himself. Another example can be seen in the stories of the American Indian 'clowns'. In *Daughters of Copperwoman*, Anne Cameron quotes an old woman of the Nootka people who live in what is now called British Columbia.

The people were goin' down to Victoria a lot and tradin' with Hudson Bay [Company] for things they couldn't get anywhere else. They'd kill seal and otter, more than ever before so they'd be able to trade the skins, and even though everyone knew it couldn't last, even though everyone knew that the animals wouldn't be able to survive, nobody seemed willin' to be the first to not do it. It was like they figured it was gonna happen anyway, they might as well get some of it for themselves. And not all the stuff they traded for was worth anythin'. You make the long trip with a big bundle of furs, and you don't feel like bringin' it all home just because the Hudson Bay man doesn't want to trade for somethin' you want. More and more the company was just handin' out junk, and private traders were steppin' in with a few blue beads and a lot of rum, it was a real mess.

And this same clown woman, she took herself down to Victoria and she set up shop right next to Hudson Bay. Hudson Bay would give beads, so she had bits of busted shell. They'd give molasses so she had wild honey. They'd give rum, so she had some old swamp water. And she just sat there. That's all she did, was just sit there. And the people goin' to Hudson Bay saw her, and the stuff she was tellin' them. Some of 'em went inside and traded anyway, but some of them just turned around and went back home, and some of them even went over and traded with her, and she treated them all real serious, took their furs and gave 'em bits of shell and stuff, and they wore it same as they'd'a wore the beads.

After a while the Hudson Bay man came out to see why hardly anybody had come to trade and he saw her sittin' there and he just about blew up, took himself off to the Governor and complained about the clown woman. The Governor, he took himself outside and had a look and then told the Hudson Bay man a thing or two, and from then on we got good tradin' stuff.

(From Anne Cameron, 1984, *Daughters of Copperwoman*, The Women's Press, London)

Following up another issue the woman set off to see the Governor and stop the rum trade. However, when she disappeared a search was made and she was found dead, shot in the head, almost certainly by a white man because the Indians never showed violence to a clown.

Nowadays this kind of role is usually taken on by the verbal stand-up comic and there are many connections between 'alternative cabaret' comics and the street equivalent. For example, Tony Allen started his career making provocative speeches at London's Hyde Park Corner. Because he used to do a lecture about obscene words he was arrested for using them. Later, in court, he was acquitted because he argued that his speech was essentially about the use of certain words. He thus played a double joke on the authorities – being arrested for simply saying 'fuck' in the first place and then getting away with pretending that he was innocently making a speech about language. In this confrontation with the authorities he wasn't particularly concerned with the audience or with making any money out of it. He simply wanted to make his point about the absurdity of certain laws. After a few years doing street theatre, Tony now works entirely in cabaret. As will be seen later, an act that is almost entirely verbal is not best suited for outdoors.

This area of work reaches its most sophisticated form in satire; the television programme *Spitting Image* is a modern example. It is important to note that for the satirists everything and everyone is liable to be the victim of their imitative ridicule, it is not their business to promote one belief system over another. The long and illustrious history of satire is better dealt with by other books but it is important to mention its street theatre version – the commedia dell'arte. All the characters in this long-lasting popular theatre were ridiculed, except for the lovers. The lovers are the fixed point in the hierarchy, above and below which there is only stupidity, pretension and the driving force of basic human passions – greed and lust. The character of the Capitano is a satire on the swaggering arrogance of a foreign occupying military; Pantalone is a combination of avaricious capitalist merchant, lecherous old man and authoritarian father; the Doctor is a satire on both the pretensions of the intellectual pedant and also the cynical self-interest of the quack doctor.

Nowadays there are different authority figures to poke fun at; Leo Bassi chooses a political orator, his sister Joanna a schoolmistress, the Natural Theatre Company use the police and reactionary protesters as targets of fun. Théâtre de l'Unité take an authoritarian event, a public execution, rather than a figure, in order to point out certain aspects of the relationship between the individual and the state. The tactic is not so much to directly oppose the authorities but on the contrary to appear to support them by imitating them. With a slight exaggeration our attention is brought to the vanity of the orator, the patronising superiority of the schoolmistress, the superciliousness of the police, the petty narrow minds of the protesters and the brutality of the state execution. Politically motivated performers sometimes make the mistake of being simply abusive about the authorities – this not only alienates large sections of the public but can often seem like the whingeing of the underdog, thus reinforcing the position of the authorities. A much better tactic is to turn the authorities into figures of fun and thus lower their status to that of clown.

Provocateurs have to be very aware of developments in society because they play on the borderline of what is acceptable. For example, Chris Lynham's total nudity has a powerful effect in the street but with other prevailing conventions he might be arrested or, if in a nudist camp, totally ignored. The circus clown dropping his trousers must have had an equally outrageous effect in the nineteenth century but, with the changes in society, this act becomes quite banal. Even at locations that are used to outdoor theatre, a watchful eye is kept on what goes on. A group called Demolition Decorators was banned from London's Covent Garden in its more liberal years, because they were 'outrageously offensive'. Nowadays all performers are obliged to undergo an audition there to see if they are 'acceptable' to perform in Covent Garden. Even at the Pompidou Centre in Paris, which is hardly a 'soft' environment, there must be a limit to how rude, nude, or political one can get before the police are called.

CHRIS LYNHAM: GOING TO THE LIMIT

Chris is another performer who started his career doing street theatre and has moved into cabaret. He has been so successful at this that in 1990 he completed a six-part TV series to which he invited other provocateurs such as Leo Bassi. He recognises the importance of street theatre in his career. 'It's a wonderful natural theatre, an ideal place to learn clowning – if the people don't like it they walk away, if it's good you make lots of money.' As he says, this can be a problem; 'Coins in bulk are heavy.' Another problem of street theatre, as he sees it, is greed – if the show is running well and making lots of money (£100 each time), the temptation is to do too many shows and burn up all energy and desire to perform. However, he says he enjoys the freedom to be able not to work if he doesn't feel like it and the ability to fly off to another country if it suits him. He doesn't like the dirtiness of performing in the streets, this is one reason he moved into cabaret. Another reason is that he feels the British street theatre scene has become too safe and predictable, it's not as original and daring as it once was.

When he worked on the streets, Chris, at one period, seemed to avoid any prepared material for a show. Everything was improvised from the situation, the environment and the audience. This is too risky to be considered by most performers

Figure 6 Chris Lynham

– sometimes it works wonderfully but at other times it fails horribly so that the act becomes too unreliable for bookers. However, these leaps into the dark have given Chris and others who have dared to follow this course a very solid grounding; he can make a show from nothing, he is always alert to the possibilities and dangers of a situation and it has given him great skill in handling his audience. It has also given him acts like his plastic bag routine which is so bizarre that it couldn't be 'thought' up but could only have arrived through an improvisation with a piece of rubbish. It is also the reason why he is so fascinating to watch. Witnessing someone who is free from inhibition, we become aware of our own fears and anxieties. We relish the feeling of liberation they give us, liberation from convention, constriction and even boring old logic. Vital people vitalise and free people liberate.

Chris's stage character starts in a baggy suit, his longish hair back-combed and fixed upright so that with his wild eyes he looks demonic. He stalks into view, staring at the audience with an expression of wicked challenge. 'The first thing I'd like to do, ladies and gentlemen . . . is go home.' This sets the tone of the performance; he doesn't give a fuck about the audience. However, the atmosphere is electric because of the sense of danger he creates. This is established and maintained throughout the show by throwing things like ice-cubes and uncooked eggs into the audience, by loud explosions and by sudden leaps into the crowd. At one point he starts undressing a member of the audience. He takes another person's shoe off and chucks it into the back of the crowd. His basic attitude is one of slow menacing threat; 'You'll wish you hadn't done that,' he says, with a devilish grin, as he approaches some plucky individual who has not done exactly as he was told.

He also creates danger by his unpredictability – sudden switches from amiable intimacy to violent mania. The undercurrent of violence explodes in unexpected acrobatics as he throws himself around or, like a jester with his inflated bladder, he hits the audience with the air-filled plastic bag. If the audience doesn't respond vocally as ordered, he threatens to throw the raw egg, building the tension of who is to be the chosen target before chucking it into the crowd. Because he carries out some of his threats he becomes very powerful. How far will he go? He pushes things to their limits; after letting the shoeless victim in the front row worry about the whereabouts of the shoe for several minutes he returns to the subject. 'The shoe returns to the stage.' It is thrown back as ordered. 'Followed by fifty other shoes!'

The rapport with the audience is established right at the beginning, he cues the audience to shout and getting no immediate reaction he snaps: 'Look do we have to go through this shit?' He cues them again and gets the desired effect. Before the shoe is chucked away he jokingly tries to auction it; demanding and receiving response, he suddenly switches the game by taking out the joke and actually demanding the money. He often includes a participation act called 'The Story of Frankie and Johnny'. This follows the usual combination of love and conflict between two men and a woman but is totally different in style; the gangster story is pushed as far as the participants are willing to go in the direction of sex and violence.

The act is not only surreal – 'Imagine you are a fish . . . how are you gonna get to the airport?' – but truly Dada in its anti-art, anti-beauty stance. A rendition of 'I Do Like To Be beside the Seaside' is sung full of hate and manic distaste. He, too, appears to be aiming to incite the spectators to riot. Like the Dadaists, however, the iconoclasm and anarchy are synthesised through a very precise artistic technique. He is always aiming to refine his physical control, the text is extremely well crafted and the order of the show well designed. He takes the piss out of art: '. . . and the plastic bag turns into Art', as he pulls out a long red silk cloth and dances with it, but the image he then creates really is beautiful. His rendition of 'Wonderful World' is sung in a hoarse, bluesy voice but is done with real feeling, only slightly ironic, all the more tender because of the character he has established.

Perhaps the part of the show that sums up his attitude and the act that he's most known for, is his rendition of 'There's No Business like Show Business'. For this he strips completely naked, puts his privates out of sight between his legs, sticks a 'Roman candle' type firework into the crack of his bum, lights it and sings the song. When performed in the streets and onstage this sometimes causes outraged protest but this only goes to prove his success as provocateur.

LEO BASSI: JUGGLER OF TABOOS

Leo Bassi is a performer who is based in Italy, although his family were travelling circus people and therefore his roots are multinational. He rarely works on the streets nowadays, doing much of his work in discothèques in Milan and elsewhere. His main work is as a mock-serious philosopher and demagogue; he founded the New Neronian Society which professes to counter the modern rational materialism with theories of cultural sensuality associated with the Emperor Nero. He is best known in Italy for his weekly TV slot as Nero.

His performances are based on a highly intelligent and articulate view of modern democratic Europe, a society without the hard edges that poverty and war gave to the world that spawned the commedia dell'arte. He therefore likes to set himself up as a figure to knock against – a paternalistic, businessman/dictator with paranoid, megalomaniac tendencies. At a pop festival in Denmark he arranged to have himself carried on to the site on a throne by a squad of real soldiers. He then set himself up in the overcrowded camping area with barbed wire and guards protecting his neat personal compound from where he taunted the festival-goers about their lack of space, their untidiness and disorganisation. This spectacle of everything they loved to hate provoked such strong feelings that his compound was invaded and he had to make a hasty comical retreat (up a tree) in order to save himself.

His work includes all types of street theatre. On one occasion he somehow managed to arrange a fly-past of Air Force jets in order to fit in with his simulation of the city being invaded. On another occasion, at the time of a crucial east-west summit, he set himself up in a cage/booth in the centre of the city as a kind of telepathic mystic who was sending benevolent vibrations to the two world leaders. He appealed to other people, by means of extensive media coverage, to join him in his mental exertions. This event obviously had its serious side but was only intended as a piece of theatre. However, hundreds of people earnestly believed him, spoke with him and prayed – a modern version of the interaction between spirituality and theatre.

His solo show for the Limburg Street Theatre Festival in 1989 was designed to be mobile, repeatable and suitable for a provincial Dutch audience. A plinth is set up in the performing area, surrounded by a little rope guard rail, Haydn's *Requiem* is playing. Into the area comes Leo Bassi, a balding middle-aged businessman with glasses and a briefcase. He moves about the space silently, sternly regarding the audience, and then climbs up on to the plinth and poses, magnificently and imperiously, occasionally looking down his nose at the assembled crowd. He does almost nothing for at least five minutes, letting the crowd get slightly impatient, preparing them to get worked up later on. If anyone comes too close to the plinth he uses his weapon – a jet of water that unexpectedly shoots out of his briefcase. Eventually he descends and addresses the crowd, using a microphone in order to enhance his status. At this stage his manner of speaking is in the grand style of politicians. His aim is not so much to entertain as to provoke, so there follows a series of acts introduced as demonstrations of a philosophical theory. He stalks round the audience holding a custard pie looking for the perfect person to suffer the indignity, in order to illustrate the ratio factor in comedy – 1 person suffers but 300 get pleasure. This stalking goes on for some time as he builds the tension, diving towards one possible candidate and then changing his mind. He is particularly keen on working up the kids in the front row, every now and again he lunges towards them so that they scream and scatter. Finally he does another lunge, stumbles and gets the pie in his own face, becoming demonically angry and ridiculous. The kids are ecstatic and start to throw spare pieces of their programmes at him. He kneels, arms outstretched in a Christ-like pose suffering the indignity to the full.

He tells the audience that he does not want them to clap but to scream instead. This raises the pitch of the performance as he continues with more confrontation; he lights a fire torch, fills his mouth with fuel and threatens to blow fire in their faces, then he produces realistic-looking shit from a bedpan and threatens to eat it in front of them. His aim is to make the audience experience something – be it fear, terror, relief, revulsion, laughter, or outrage – rather than just watching in the passive, detached way they can watch television. Here is a real live human being who can make direct physical and emotional contact, pushing people to their limits of acceptability, and working the kids up to near hysteria. It is not so much a show, more an incitement to riot. One would think that many of the public would be so offended by his use of emotive subjects, like cruelty to children, car

Figure 7 Leo Bassi charms the children

accidents and shit-eating, that they would walk away, but every-one becomes fascinated, eager to see whatever will happen next.

Towards the end of his act, just when we feel that it is all getting too much, he switches to an astonishing couple of foot-juggling acts, one with large silver balls and the other with a box in the shape of an upright piano, which he tosses, balances and rotates. Once again the pretext is to illustrate a point. 'Juggling', he says, 'makes me feel very sad. When I think of all the tragedy and suffering in the world I wonder how I could have wasted so much time and energy learning such a frivolous and useless activity.' He is, in fact, one of the best foot-jugglers in Europe. He ends the show with another speech, addressing the host town like a visiting politician; referring to their past history and to their future in a united Europe in which there will be more people like him from the south coming to incite their children and mess up the town square.

He never comes across as merely aggressive or crude, it is all done with a certain calculated finesse. There is, however, a real sense of danger – will anybody speak out against him, take their children away in disgust, or even put a stop to the show? Danger and threat are his tools to provoke. Sometimes he will start a show with an earth-shattering explosion; with that he establishes that he means business. Surprisingly at the Limburg Festival performance the older people who might have been offended were very respectful not only of the skills but also of his intel-ligence and underlying motivation. They were more concerned that he had been offended by the over-excited and playfully abusive children.

THE NATURAL THEATRE COMPANY: THE ART OF MISCHIEF

The Natural Theatre Company is one of the most well-established street theatre companies in Europe. They have been at it for over twenty-one years, performing all over the world, often with several teams operating at the same time. Their speciality is walkabout theatre but they also perform indoor theatre shows and animate site-specific journeys. Because of their pre-eminence their work is referred to frequently within this book. A fuller description of their work will be given in the section on mobile shows but for now it is worth looking at them in the context of provocateurs.

The following is an extract from an interview with Ralph Oswick, their co-founder and mentor.

We are mischievous, you see, and we've always got our eye on what's going on. We think: That needs deflating, or: We've got exactly the right characters to go and appear there. We try not to do it in isolation; like the meeting with Maggie Thatcher that was in every newspaper. We were in the flower show and there are ways of finding out where they are going to be and hanging about there in a harmless way. Wearing something like that [huge flower pots over their heads], they can't get rid of you; even the heaviest security man hasn't got the nerve to rip the mask off in case you're supposed to be there.

We met Maggie as nannies at Expo. We tried to meet every world leader that came. We chose something that would fit so we put little nodding Maggie Thatcher dolls in our prams. The security man came and said, 'I'm afraid you're not supposed to be here', and I said, well Nanny said, 'On the contrary young man, this is exactly where we are supposed to be. We've been told to be here and we've been told we mustn't be anywhere else.' He went away and came back later pointing to an enormous-shouldered bloke and said, 'That young man over there says that you're definitely not supposed to be here and you must go', and I said, 'Well that young man will find he hasn't got a job in the morning.' So he went away again and this went on for some time until Maggie arrived and Denis said, 'Oh look!' and they all came rushing over and NTC is immediately in newspapers all over the world. A large, butch, lady security woman was the only one that dared take the plunge in the end and she was last seen pushing one of our prams away along this avenue of cheering people and you could see she wished she'd never laid hands on it. None of the blokes would have pushed a pram, they couldn't, they can wrest an automatic weapon off somebody but they could never dare to push a pram along, especially if they thought: Perhaps they are meant to be there and I haven't been told.

So it's sort of mischief really. When you're doing it

Figure 8 The Natural Theatre's protesters making audience contact

you've got to have two minds; you're doing the character but at the same time you're looking for the next opportunity.

On another occasion, at the Dublin Festival, they made a point about the exclusion of all the performers from the gala night; only politicians, sponsors, arts organisers and sundry rich and famous were invited. They bluffed their way in by turning up in a Rolls at the same time as all the other VIPs and doing a totally convincing imitation of a 'famous person', her consort and their personal security guards. They walked straight in, past the armed police, and were mingling happily with cabinet ministers and the like before being discovered and hustled out. This took a lot of explaining in the police station but received the publicity they wanted in order to make their point.

As already mentioned, they sometimes choose authority figures to imitate and thereby subtly subvert. One of their pieces is a walkabout investigation by a group of dour-faced British policemen and policewomen led by a cliché, pipe-smoking detective in a brown mackintosh. Like another of their pieces, 'The Egghead Aliens', their attitude to the environment is one of silent observation. They play with the powerful effect of the uniform – they are mildly threatening and will suddenly search people, take drinks away for inspection (and surreptitious consumption), sniff cigarettes and look at everyone with a cold air of suspicion. The uniform gives them a high status which they use to control the public with a derogatory flick of a pointed finger. However, once this status has been established, they subtly undermine the cold inhuman approach with very human weaknesses; while frisking someone they start to get a bit sensual, in testing a drink or cigarette for clues they show a flicker of enjoyment. At a famous episode at the Glastonbury Festival a policeman and a policewoman were observed snogging passionately on the grass. This is a very gentle but very acute form of subversion of authority and in so doing can alter our perception of our guardians of law and order.

Another piece involves a number of very normal people in out-of-date clothes, brown macs, suits, and trilby hats. They carry placards saying 'Down with Bicycles' and 'Pedal Power? No Thanks!'. They march down the street like a mini-protest, forming a line at suitable locations such as a bicycle repair shop. Coming across a line of parked bicycles they 'sabotage' them by laying them on their side. Sometimes they will avoid and sneer at bicycle-owners, other times they will confront them, pulling at their pannier straps, or laying lines of drawing pins in their path. Occasionally they take more extreme and ludicrous measures by lying down in front of them. A cyclist who pedals away may be chased by these placard-wielding objectors. Although there is a confrontation it is gentle, never verbal and as far as possible spread amongst a whole group rather than focused on a few individuals. What they seem to be trying to achieve is to make fun of self-righteous reactionary forces but also to provoke the spectators into expressing their opposition to these characters, safe in the knowledge that it is only a game.

Chapter 6

Communicators

Provocateurs make fun of personal taboos and the conventions of society but, as already mentioned, they do not identify themselves with a particular ideological standpoint. They debunk rather than promote ideas. In a sense theirs is an easier role than that of the communicators, whose aim is not so much to provoke a particular group of spectators but to criticise certain aspects of the wider society. Communicators may even take it upon themselves to advocate a particular ideology or course of action, which might be moral, religious, or political. Because there is often a desire to convey a clear unequivocal message, complex themes are often simplified into conflicts of good versus evil, whether in terms of devils tempting saints or oppressors oppressing the oppressed. More recently, technology has become the popular baddie with simple humanity and the environment as the victims. They often tackle specific current issues, representing contemporary life and, by means of their interpretation, making a comment upon it. In some political theatre this comment was boldly stated, but this 'agit-prop' method tended to alienate because most people recoil from such a blunt approach. Nowadays 'agit-prop' has been dropped in favour of a more subtle approach, so that the audience has more room to draw its own conclusions, even if it has been carefully manipulated.

Either way, theatre, in this case, is being used as an educational tool. As educators, these performers feel they have something to teach to the rest of society, a message to pass on, or at least a need to draw society's attention to issues that it prefers to ignore. By implication, they feel they have a more complete understanding of a particular situation than the rest of society.

These communicators can be found throughout most art forms but they have often used street theatre as a means to reach ordinary people.

There are two strands to communicator theatre. The first is to reinforce, affirm and encourage the already converted. In this case, because it can be assumed that there is prior knowledge, a shorthand of images can be used suggestive of larger ideas; the cross, for example, is a symbol of the meeting of heaven and earth as well as a reminder of the crucifixion. The hammer and sickle represents the union of agricultural and industrial workers. Portraits of saints or political leaders are a reminder of their ideas and their life stories. As well as visual images, music too can help reinforce a message. Songs have long been associated with communicators, whether religious, nationalist, or political, since they combine text with emotional uplift through the music. Because of background noise in the streets too much text, spoken or sung, can be a problem.

The second strand is to do with drawing attention to an issue or persuading an unconverted audience to see society differently. The problem here is how to engage the audience. To do this communicators always use the most popular mediums available. Political revolutionaries have used popular forms such as folk theatre, music hall and circus, often producing an interesting result as educated intellectuals reinvent the old formats. Nowadays, advertisers use television to demonstrate their fantastic variety of tactics. Traditionally the simplest and most popular medium was story-telling. Stories enable an emotional involvement with the issue that can be much more powerful than simply appealing to the intellect. All world religions use story-telling as a means to explain spiritual ideas; Jesus and Buddha used parables and later on the stories from their lives became the illustration of their message. Even today, advertisers frequently use mini-stories to engage the public and communicate their message.

In the Middle Ages the church authorities used the visual image by mounting living tableaux on carts and wheeling them round town in order to illustrate scenes from the Bible. Later on they developed this idea into story-telling by putting the scenes into a coherent sequence. The narrative was fleshed out by dialogue to produce the mystery and miracle plays. Nativity plays are still being used in this way to teach children the

Christmas story. Communicator groups such as Welfare State and Mummer & Dada use the mummers' story of death versus life with its celebratory rebirth ending.

The problem of presenting stories in the streets is that it is important that the audience watches the whole piece from beginning to end, so communicators will tend to organise a pre-arranged time and place for the show rather than using the more informal arrangements that are possible for other types of performer. In this type of theatre, the main dramatic opposition is between protagonists or forces within the piece and not between the audience and performer. This is the fundamental difference between this group and provocateurs. Usually communicators cannot maintain continuous contact with the audience because, whether using a narrative or not, the protagonists will be caught up in other relationships than that with the public. If a narrative is used there may be a 'fourth wall' effect with the actors pretending they are in a different space from the audience, even though there may also be points within the show designed to include the audience. If a separate reality is being created onstage, in this way, any interruptions can distract and undermine, so many communicators tend to use stationary shows because this means that there will be fewer uncontrollable variations that might interrupt the sequence. It also means that a pre-fixed set, lighting and sound equipment can support the illusion. Even Boal's ferry-boat journey (a good example of educative theatre), described earlier (p. 6), was, in a sense, a mobile stationary show since the audience and environment were contained and controllable. Because stories are easier with more than two performers, this type of theatre is usually done by groups.

With all these considerations it can be seen that the criteria are not so very different from indoor theatre and many artists of this type have strong connections with indoor theatre of one sort or another. These groups usually organise shows with a short life-span rather than developing one show over a number of years, as is usually the case with entertainers, animators and provocateurs. Apart from considerations of scale, the main difference from indoor theatre is that the narrative is conveyed through visual images rather than words, although, with the introduction of radio microphones, groups such as Generik Vapeur and Welfare State are able to complement their large visual images with spoken or sung text. So although the outdoor environment is not the natural home of communicators they choose to try to surmount the difficulties because they want to convey their ideas to a public that might not be easily tempted to go indoors.

COVENT GARDEN COMMUNITY THEATRE

As already stated, there is nowadays very little political theatre outdoors in Britain. One of the most successful in its time was Covent Garden Community Theatre. The group was formed in the mid-1970s to voice protest about the commercial redevelopment of London's Covent Garden area in a classic homes-versus-offices issue and later on a homes-versus-wine-bars issue. After these were resolved, they dealt with the wider themes of capitalism, the workings of Parliament and other subjects such as the effects of the new communication technologies, nuclear power and pollution. These less localised issues enabled them to tour outside London to the country festivals and to the continent.

Having decided on a theme they would spend considerable time deciding what was the fundamental issue and which were related back-up issues so that each was presented in the right proportion. They found that, in order to avoid alienating the public, they had to be very careful about naming the issue. One example was when dealing with the subject of squatting. Squatters were not popular with the working-class community, so they simply drew attention to the absentee landlords making a profit on empty properties, properties which could have made good homes for 'young families in the area'.

The shows were designed to fit into the tight corners of pubs and community centres as well as for the streets, tents and fields. They combined the uncompromising extreme contrasts of agit-prop (for example, juxtaposing the fortunes of a woman cleaner with those of the Queen), with a high level of entertaining skills, particularly music, puppetry and magic, all laced with a well-developed sense of humour. Fortunately, they found that the workings of local government, far from being as tedious as one might expect, were often quite ludicrous and a perfect subject for comedy, if presented in the right way.

Working in pubs was often an uphill task as they tried to be heard above the uninterested, noisy people at the bar, so they had to develop their skills fast. Mindful of the way some contemporary political theatre groups harangued their audience and made them recoil, they found that puppets were extremely effective at stopping people in their tracks and drawing them in. Their style managed to combine story-telling with cabaret and the simple, direct statement of facts and figures. A characteristic example of their style was the way they found to illustrate the rather tedious interconnection of various committees, draft schemes and area plans. These were shown in the form of rolls of paper, linked by means of strings, into the shape of a skeleton, and this was revealed step by step to an adaptation of the song 'Dem Bones, Dem Bones'.

Far from simply reworking old political themes, they were often very accurate in their assessment of the implications of the innovations of the Thatcher years. For example, in 1979 they showed us a micro-chip and warned that this tiny object would transform our lives. It hardly seemed possible at the time.

LICIDEI'S CLOWN APOCALYPSE

Licidei is a Russian clown group based in Moscow. In the years preceding the glasnost era there was a healthy tradition of circus clowning in Russia that provided one of the few means of making fun of the authoritarian system. Licidei grew out of this tradition, but because of their challenging perspective they remained on the fringes of wide public exposure, gradually building up a strong following on the underground scene. With the dramatic changes in government policy they received official backing and were able to mount large outdoor processions and spectacles and to travel abroad. In the summer of 1989, before the removal of the Berlin Wall, they were involved in the Mir Caravan project (mir means 'peace' in Russian) – a collection of ten well-established theatre groups from both east and west Europe that performed and travelled together from Moscow and Leningrad to Prague, Warsaw and cities in western Europe. Their outdoor spectacle, 'Catastrophe', was based on the disaster at Chernobyl but, rather than making a direct representation of that particular event, they created another technological disaster which was done in their own inimitable style. It seems an unusual subject for a clown group to tackle but it is only in the west that we tend to think of red-nosed clowns as unconnected to the grim reality of the modern world.

The show was done at night by seven performers. The audience was arranged on three sides of a square with clearly marked boundaries for reasons of safety. The fourth side was reserved for vehicles mounted with lights and other equipment. At each of the corners a flaming oil barrel provided light and smoke which set up an atmosphere of desolate wasteland before the beginning of the show.

It starts with a clown master of ceremonies making an incomprehensible speech to the crowd in a manner that is half politician and half television compere. We gather that some kind of great technological experiment is about to take place which involves a wheelbarrow race. The brave 'pilots' of the wheelbarrows are introduced like departing astronauts. They wear white crash helmets and military greatcoats and have parachutes slung on their chests. The build-up is long as everything needs to be carefully prepared; just as all seems ready, an old-soldier clown on crutches appears and takes the microphone, warning of the dangers and pleading with them to stop the experiment. He is brushed aside but when he insists, the microphone is wrenched off him and his crutches kicked so that he falls.

All is now prepared and the master of ceremonies ignites parallel lines of petrol-soaked sawdust. With a starting pistol and a wave of a flag, the signal to commence is given. The three pilots advance with their wheelbarrows down the flaming race-track and have almost reached the end when coloured smoke starts billowing from one wheelbarrow and this careers off-course and crashes into another, which also starts to smoke until all three are zig-zagging out of control around the arena. A loud wailing siren is set off and other clowns start running in all directions – clown stretcher bearers, others with fire-extinguishers, which add to the confusion as figures disappear into the clouds of gas and smoke. Fire-crackers and larger explosions start to be heard intermittently. One of the pilots unfurls his parachute which is inflated horizontally from a large industrial fan. Another pilot has coloured smoke pouring from his costume as he staggers around the space looking for help. Other flares are lit as the panic continues. The old soldier limps around trying to help and bewailing the stupidity of the experiment but is again knocked off his crutches in the confusion.

In the distance another siren can be heard, that of a real fire-engine. It gets closer and suddenly appears. The crowd is forced to move by the panic-stricken clowns and the fire-engine, with its blue rotating lights, enters the space. Hoses are detached but, instead of water coming out, a billowing sea of foam is created, standing up to a metre deep on the ground. The different sorts of flame and electric light filtering through the smoke, parachute and foam produce extraordinary effects of silhouette, back-lighting and dazzle. The wall of foam slowly advances, engulfing the entire area as the figures get caught up and have difficulty extricating themselves from it. They struggle with it, slowly getting sucked under; the old soldier falls silent gazing at the apocalyptic scene until he too is drowned.

The clown style not only helped in the transformation of this tragic sequence but added to its poignancy. The military clowns were shown to be just as stupid as the more obviously comic stretcher-bearer duo. All were naive except for the old soldier, whose cruel treatment and despair were tragi-comic and extremely moving. If it had not been done by clowns the representation might have been more naturalistic but too heavy-handed, with no light human touches to counterbalance the dark theme. If we can laugh at the pathetic, foolish clowns we can also cry with them at the extent of human folly.

Chapter 7

Performing artists

For the purposes of this book, performing artists are defined as those whose main concern is to create interesting visual images. They tend to be painters and sculptors first and performers second. 'Performance Art' is a more specific term to describe those whose main preoccupations are time, space, chance, juxtaposition and the subconscious. Performance artists may be communicators but what they wish to communicate is about the nature of art or about visual perception. If they want to shock, like provocateurs, then it is usually the artistic elite who are their targets, not ordinary people in the street. There may be a degree of audience participation but only as one element in the total concept; the artist is not interested in the individual personalities of the participants. There is a strong current of misanthropy evident in the line of development from the futurists and Dada. The only connection with entertainment is the perennial interest they have in circus, fairground and cabaret, partly because these lack narrative and meaning and also juxtapose contrasting disciplines. With the current mixing of styles, much of Performance Art has became absorbed into the rest of 'experimental' theatre.

The performing artists who work outdoors try to make their work accessible, often with an element of comedy. They may simply want to make the drab, harsh streets a more beautiful and joyful place. Often their work is fantastical and, to a communicator or provocateur, might even seem escapist. As visual artists they see the outside world as an interesting setting for their work or even the inspiration of the work itself; they therefore frequently do work that is site-specific. Even if they tour a pre-rehearsed set-piece they try to leave it very flexible in order to be able to use the physical aspects of each different location. This means they have a more rapid turnover of material than the communicators. As visual artists they are obviously concerned with the effects of lighting and so often develop a taste for pyrotechnics. They are not so concerned with drama, storytelling, or a direct relationship with the audience, so the sequence of the images is often worked out only after they have been developed.

Like communicators, they want to confront a general public with their work and themselves be confronted by an unsophisticated response. Unlike communicators, however, there is no 'message', they are more concerned with form than content, while acknowledging that the two are inseparable. As the manifesto of Dogtroep puts it:

> Our art is not a vehicle for morality, our images are not symbols which tell you something you cannot see . . . We are not interested in an objective art production – which you can occasionally see on video – but one which the spectator experiences during the performance and which remains afterwards. . . . Art is not about masterpieces but about how art functions. The most important thing about a work of art is what it evokes in the thoughts and feelings of the spectator.

The activity of painters or sculptors is essentially different from that of performers because they strive to satisfy their own aesthetic sense first and the feedback from other spectators is secondary to the relationship of the artist and the work. The Dogtroep manifesto again:

> The overall effect of the performance is the result of the obsessions and whims of the individuals of the company . . . Dogtroep does what it likes. Dogtroep seeks, finds and develops markets which will pay it to do what it likes.

Painters and sculptors will be happy if their work has a wide appeal but they will probably be more concerned with the response of a limited number of people whose opinions they respect. Performance, on the other hand, has got to appeal to a wider public at a specific moment in time. In the same way that communicators are likely to have had some training in drama, the visual artists who work in outdoor theatre are often from an art school background so that the spectators can take it or leave it according to their taste and inclination, as in a gallery situation. This means that contact with the audience will be very limited. It also means that in creating the piece the response of the audience is not the main concern. The danger with this attitude is that it leads to the elitist approach described earlier; for many years inaccessible Performance Art was supported by like-minded *cognoscenti* who were influential in securing public subsidy and so it survived despite an almost total lack of popular support. The positive side of this lack of concern with the immediate response was that a lot of brave experimentation was done for its own sake. This produced some of the delightfully eccentric types of performance that are no longer being produced. Nowadays the importance of popular appeal is tending to produce less challenging work from the new generation of performers.

Many of today's performing artists have been influenced by previous collaborations between theatre and visual art, one example of which were the seventeenth-century masque performances. In these, stage machinery was invented that could reproduce effects for the fantastic classical and allegorical stories that were in vogue. The costumes, sets, lighting and stage effects were more important than the performers. Usually the performance was integrated with a grand ball. Because these masques were so expensive to produce, they were staged only in royal palaces and were often like elaborate amateur theatricals with the royal person taking the starring part. Louis XIV in particular was fond of playing this role.

Another example is the tradition of creating large visual images in the form of pageants. These were descendants of the religious pageants and seasonal folk traditions that were common before the Reformation. In later times they were used to celebrate royal visits or military victories even up until the end of the First World War. They involved the decoration of wagons as a backdrop for living tableaux much like the modern carnival float. More importantly, the town was decorated and temporary structures such as triumphal arches were erected. In 1987 the Welsh theatre company Brith Gof was involved in the decoration of the village of Llanrhaeadr to celebrate the four-hundredth anniversary of the Welsh Bible. They used thirty-two huge, beautifully decorated banners which were strategically placed around the village. More radical is the work of Donato Sartori, son of the great leather-mask maker Amleto Sartori, whose group, Centro Maschere, aims to put a 'mask' on the cityscape by using plastic fibres that are stretched over a suitable main square like an enormous spider's web.

A more important influence for today's performing artists were the events of the futurists, Dadaists and surrealists. These greatly influenced those who organised the 'happenings' of the 1960s. Hans Richter, the veteran Dada artist, describes a happening in New York in 1962 which he recognised as being very much in the spirit of Dada.

The 'Happening' I went to see took place in the enormous courtyard of a skyscraper, the Mills Hotel in the Village. This is the biggest 'flophouse' in the world, twelve hundred little rooms for the poorest of the poor, who still have to pay 50 cents a night. In the middle of this courtyard, this immense chasm, Alan Kaprow and his assistants had built a high scaffold about five storeys high, covered with black paper, cardboard and sacks. Two ladders gave access to the platform on top. High in the air, many floors above this scaffold, hung an immense dome, also covered in black.

About two hundred spectators lined the walls of this dream-prison. Hundreds looked down at us from little barred windows hardly a foot and a half across. Then we were issued with brooms and the 'audience' began to sweep the ground, which was covered with newspapers and other litter. When all was clean, black charred scraps of paper showered down out of the sky to the accompaniment of wailing sirens and someone blowing a trumpet. More paper rained down, empty sacks and cardboard boxes began to fall out of the night sky . . . and we noticed a cyclist who was very slowly riding round and round and round the giant scaffold, and who continued to do so all evening. A motor-tyre on the end of a cable swung out of a corner high above us and knocked some large cardboard boxes (which had fallen from the dome) off the top of the scaffold and down on to the spectators. An Ophelia in white began to dance, with a transistor radio held to her ear, round the scaffold that now looked like a sacrificial altar. After several circuits she climbed up the ladder to the platform five storeys up. Fearful noise of sirens. She was immediately followed by two photographers, who climbed up the two ladders after her. Half-way up, one of them lost his camera and had to go back and fetch it. Up above, Ophelia was photographed in provocative poses; only her legs were visible from below. Deluges of paper, thunder-effects, howlings and screechings, and the dome began to sink slowly until it had covered Ophelia, photographers, cardboard boxes and motor-tyre. The sacrifice was at an end.

(Hans Richter, *Dada – Art and Anti-Art*,
pp. 212–13)

Performing outdoors has forced the performing artists to be accountable to audience reaction. There is little satisfaction in creating art that your chosen type of audience has little interest in. All of the groups that have survived have done so because they tempered their very serious, self-conscious approach with a sense of humour. Humour takes the pretension out of the work and informs the public that the show is meant to be enjoyed in a light-hearted way. Otherwise the general public is left with a feeling of inadequacy because they do not understand a piece that may not have been intended to have 'meaning'.

FORKBEARD FANTASY

Forkbeard Fantasy are a good example of this light-hearted performance art. They are a trio, based in Devon. The performers are two brothers, Tim and Chris Britton, who were joined by the puppet constructor Penny Saunders in 1980. They mainly work inside theatres but, since they enjoy direct contact with a fresh public, they maintain a certain amount of outdoor work. Their 'Great British Square Dance' has been described earlier (p. 22). Their more recent outdoor piece is 'The Red Strimmers' – a couple of workmen dressed completely in red to contrast with the park environment for which the show was devised. They are equipped with various strange contraptions that are used as portable, mechanised gardening aids. For example, they have an advanced type of 'pooper scooper' that is made from an electric fan and the motor of a windscreen wiper. This rather inefficient device creates a drama between object and actor that can be safely observed at a distance and helps to arouse people's curiosity and draw them in. At first there is little interaction with the public but gradually the performers improvise with them, explaining the prototype nature of the new equipment and sharing with them the problems of technology. Because they play it absolutely seriously, nobody is quite sure if they are real or not. 'They try to look behind our eyes', as Tim Britton put it. The gadgetry looks totally convincing and lends them credibility for who would go to the trouble of inventing and constructing useless tools? Another contraption has the ostensible purpose of spraying the tops of trees and consists of a long extending tube that is strapped to the waist and cranked up into position like an enormous phallus. When the required water pressure has been achieved by a pumping action, at the crucial orgasmic moment, the operator is distracted, rotates and sprays the crowd with the emitted fluid. This action produces hoots of laughter, particularly from older women, and especially because the characters are so male, efficient and serious about the whole business.

DOGTROEP

Dogtroep is the foremost outdoor theatre group in Holland. They have recently begun to do more indoor work but they are best known for their extensive work outdoors or in unusual locations such as abandoned churches, warehouses, factories and railway stations. They began in 1975 and spent the first ten years experimenting with different formats and techniques, creating a solid foundation for their increasing international success in the last six years. They are now offered three times as much work as they are able to do.

Fortunately, they document their work extremely well so it is possible to let them describe it directly. The artistic director, Warner van Wely, explains something of their origins.

Our main influence is English performance theatre by groups like People Show, John Bull and IOU. And especially Welfare State – I worked on and off with them for three years. We've not just learned from their artistic ideas, but also from the way they are, or were, organised. Before I started with Dogtroep I had to make a decision. At that time there was the physical theatre based on Grotowski and Open Theater, which was very intensive. But I felt that the people were wrapped up in a world of their own. We preferred the English groups which were extremely open and easy-going with the audience.

Like IOU and Welfare State, the workers are not divided into designers, constructors, musicians and actors.

All Dogtroep players are familiar with all the techniques used in performance; the designers are the producers and the performers.

However, first and foremost they are image makers; this means that in the performance the actions are 'done' rather than 'acted'. The integration of roles means that there are always new ideas being produced and tried out, often stimulated by the different locations.

Dogtroep does not have any regular productions; it combines scenes worked out on location with existing material to produce constantly fresh performances. . . . Every performance is part of the stream of performances. It's not so much the performance itself which matters so much to us as the changing elements which can be arranged in different ways.

This means that it is difficult to encapsulate their work with a description of one performance. It is also difficult to describe a specific performance adequately because the impact is through the extraordinary visual images and sound rather than in the specific actions. However, it seems important to try.

In the summer of 1989, Dogtroep were touring a show entitled 'Special II'. When this was performed at the Limburg Festival the audience was arranged around the edges of a clearly demarcated square space about 35 metres across.

The space is virtually empty except for a polythene tent-like structure in one corner. From behind the crowd an odd two-tone sound is heard, the source of which circumnavigates the outside perimeter of the crowd before stepping into the space. It is two men with extraordinary geometric make-up and costumes, one has a cow bell, the other has an odd contraption of two wooden organ pipes strapped to his back. Into these he

blows air by means of bellows attached to each arm. The insistent rhythm thus created is then complemented by them wailing
a chant reminiscent of the singing of east Europe and north
Africa. Percussive and other Asian-sounding music accompanies
the rest of the performance. They circle the inside of the perimeter like mummers warming up the enclosed space. As they go
round another extraordinary figure, wearing an inverted conical hat and a conical skirt, appears from one corner. He is
heaving on a rope and, as he progresses further into the space,
the rope appears longer and longer; it is only when he has
disappeared into the other corner that the object of his labours is
revealed. It is a rough, welded, scrap-metal dog on wheels. As
the dog continues its lone voyage across the empty space, odd
black and white shapes can be seen floating around inside the
aquarium-like polythene tent.

An opening appears and out comes a woman wearing a huge
insect-like creature, 3 metres long, on her head. It is mottled
with black and white patches like those of a Friesian cow. Her
costume is of the same design and she carries two smaller insect
creatures and places them carefully. Other similar women
appear bringing more. These are 'flown' around the space until
there is another commotion from outside the area. Two figures
can be seen over the heads of the crowd, high up on a structure
that begins to move forward. The crowd is ushered aside and an
enormous long cart, with wheels 2 metres high, is pulled into the
space with much frantic activity by a team of technicians and
performers. They attach it to the centre of the cross structure
that had provided the frame of the tent, now denuded of its
polythene. The ensemble is then heaved into a vertical position
so that it looks a bit like a windmill. Meanwhile, the insects have
disappeared and a box-frame pig with long thin legs appears. It
is someone on stilts, concealed inside the frame, with two poles
as forelegs. Suddenly a mini racing car roars into the space and
confronts the pig. The pig kicks it. The car retreats, the pig
advances and kicks again. The driver gets out and proceeds to
amputate the legs of the pig with an electric saw. It hobbles
away. A short fat husband and wife appear; wide hoops disguise
their crouched position. One has a pet dragon, which grows
wings and flies off (the puppet is lifted on very long poles).

The performance has been carefully timed so that by this time
it is beginning to get dark. The top of the windmill structure is

Figure 9 Dogtroep in 'Special II'

tilted so that the cross-bars are horizontal. Four of the performers attach themselves to the ends of these so that they hang
suspended in mid-air, astride large conga drums which have
lights inside them, illuminating their faces. Another performer
pulls a rope to rotate the upper structure so that the drummers
swing out to the side. Finally lines of petrol-soaked sawdust, on
the ground, are ignited while two or three performers rotate a
cross-frame of long fire torches. A huge vertical jet of water
from a fire-hose finishes the performance, cascading down to
extinguish the flames which are the only remaining light source.
There is darkness and silence before the applause.

Except for the arguing couple and the pig sequence, there are
hardly any relationships between the elements. Apart from the
factor of increasing darkness, the sequence of images could be
rearranged without seriously spoiling the effect. Many of the
spectators look for meaning, and are left wondering.

You can look at our performances in different ways. You
can try to see a meaning in everything, but you'll soon get
lost if you try. Still, I don't think this bothers any of the
spectators, because something different happens each
time. You might compare it with day-dreaming: thinking
without bothering about your thoughts, letting something
unimportant in, which suddenly assumes importance . . .

If you create a mass of conditions before you can tell a
story, you get a narrative that depends on all kinds of
frames of reference. People need prior information to
understand what you're saying. What we're doing has to be
exciting for every group of people.

Images don't have a definite, underlying meaning. I
don't believe in symbols. For instance, in a piece of street
theatre we did some eight years ago, we created a minia-
ture landscape on a cart with palm trees, where four well-
dressed gentlemen relaxed with a book and a pipe. We had
a bird figure who ran around it, pushing the cart forward
and blowing a horn to drive people out of the way. You
think that up, elitist artist that you are. But then you put it
on in a shopping centre, and there's an immediate feedback from the public who are doing their shopping. Then
you can hear that they see a lot in it: the people are the
bird's prisoners, they are imprisoned in reading their

books. Others say: the bird is the slave of the men, he is at
their beck and call. We're not concerned to argue one side
or the other, we create ambiguous, hermetic images which
you can hang meaning on, but which don't have any meaning themselves.
    An image doesn't have a single meaning. We make im-
ages which *are able* to suggest a lot. Feature films usually
have a dramaturgical structure, but what sticks in people's
minds are the images. A landscape crossed by a man on a
horse. You can work more directly with images. Perhaps
the dramaturgical structure is a pretext to show the images.

We live in an information age; the communication technologies provide us with a never-ending stream of images to read.
TV advertising has educated us to read a 'shorthand' of images
so that we pick up the message within the minimum amount of
time. It becomes increasingly hard for us to let images exist by
themselves without our projecting a meaning into them – just to
watch without reading. In these conditions it is very hard for
groups like Dogtroep to go against the powerful mainstream.
They have been confronted with rejection but have won
through with their unflagging dedication and refusal to compro-
mise. Their presentation is deliberately not slick, despite the fact
that this is a problem for some spectators. If the audience can
get over this block and forget about searching for literal meaning they can begin to appreciate the fantastic imagination and
ingenuity that are of increasing value in this logic-obsessed
world.

STALKER STILTS

Stalker Stilts is an Australian group. It comprises three stilt-
dancers and three musicians who play keyboards, percussion
and brass instruments. The dancers have a very high level of
skill on the stilts and are clearly well trained in acrobatics and
dance. This enables them to do hand- and head-stands with the
stilts on and to have the astonishing capacity to get up off
the ground unaided. The show consists, quite simply, of three
carefully choreographed movement pieces. In the first piece
they hold poles which are covered within a one-piece costume
that also covers their faces and the rest of their body so

that it looks as if they have long, insect-like arms. They remove this costume for the second part so that they are unhindered getting on and off the ground to perform their acrobatic balances and rolls. In the third part they use a number of multi-coloured flags to make various patterns.

Figure 10 Stalker Stilts

There is very little attempt to make any drama out of the relationships between the three of them, although at one point there is a kind of martial-art confrontation with long poles. The performance is much more concerned with spatial relationships and the extraordinary shapes that they can create with their extended legs. It is like a sculptural kaleidoscope, the different positions constantly changing to create new spatial interactions. As well as the visual art aspect, it also works as an entertaining spectacle because everyone marvels at their skill and flexibility, holding these difficult positions and performing what seem impossible moves. One of the commonly voiced objections to Performance Art is that it seems too easy – anyone can do weird things and call it art – but Stalker Stilts have clearly done a considerable amount of training and have found an original way to combine a skill, which is normally thought of in a circus context, with modern dance and sculpture.

Part II

Ways and means

WHY OUTDOORS?

In Part I we have discussed the various reasons why performers choose to work outdoors. In Part III we look at how they achieve their various aims. Before examining their different methods, it is worth looking at what all outdoor performers share in common, as compared with indoor theatre.

Indoor theatre provides a much more supportive environment. The lights and absence of unwelcome sounds enable a much more total theatrical illusion; they also give a focus which makes possible greater subtlety and emotional depth. The audience is comfortably seated and is unlikely to leave before the end. Without this support and security the outdoor performer is much more exposed to unpredictable conditions and the harsher judgement of an audience that can walk away.

However, there are an immediacy and intimacy possible outdoors. Even in a cabaret situation, where heckling and improvisation are common, the glare of the lights, the microphone and the edge of the stage all set the performer apart. With lights shining in the eyes it is hard to see the audience and so contact and interaction are harder. Outdoors the changing conditions and interruptions mean that each performance is a unique event whereas indoor performances tend to be more of an easily repeatable product. Repetition encourages fine-tuning but the lack of flexibility can lead to mechanical, uninspired performing. The outdoor performer cannot get away without energy and spirit.

The other main advantage of outdoor theatre is the possibility of using quite different materials, locations and effects. With no roof, walls, or fixed seating to limit the possibilities, whole new areas of scale are opened up. On a simple level jugglers can throw their clubs as high as they want, on a larger scale Royal de Luxe can send up a hot-air balloon, on an even bigger scale Welfare State can build a vast set and then set fire to it, accompanied by a dazzling firework display. Water too can be used, either in the way Dogtroep have shown (see p. 136) or mixed with air and detergent to make vast amounts of foam, as used by groups like Licidei and Scharlaten. Large-scale events can use cranes, bulldozers, boats and even trains, all quite impossible to use indoors although 'new' circuses such as Archaos are using some of these types of effects.

The advantages of particular locations are employed to varying degrees but no outdoor theatre would miss an opportunity to make use of a favourable setting. Other groups, doing site-specific work, design their shows for each particular location. This means that rivers, bridges, beaches, waterfalls, woods, warehouses and even railway yards can not only enrich the drama but become its subject.

For practical purposes outdoor theatre can be divided into three areas: stationary shows, mobile shows and site-specific work which can be both mobile and stationary.

Chapter 8

The stationary show

CHOOSING A SPACE

Just as one would carefully consider the possibilities of lighting, set and acoustics in an indoor theatre, so too one must look at an outdoor location with the same criteria in mind. A few yards down the street can make all the difference.

A plain wall immediately behind is extremely important. It not only helps prevent theft of props and equipment but also bounces sound back to the audience. Even the side of a marquee or a thick hedge is better than nothing. It is best not to come too far away from this wall otherwise the crowd will tend to creep in at the back. Having a back wall will also avoid too much distraction behind. At one festival we played at, we had no choice but to back on to a low fence with trapeze classes going on behind us; every now and then we could see the audience's attention being caught by a drama different from the one we were trying to create. Another time we were asked to perform backing directly on to busy Hackney High Street. Not only would we not have been heard, but also we would have had passing double-decker buses and their gaping passengers as a visual background. It is difficult for an audience and a performer to cope with that amount of distraction, although it is not absolutely impossible if the work is visual enough.

The more neutral the back wall the better; it is difficult to transform the space if the show is dominated by a huge advertisement. Sometimes there is no other option than to perform in front of a shop window; usually the proprietors don't mind as long as their customers are not obstructed. Banks or other institutions that don't need to display their wares often have plain walls and are less likely to take much notice of what is happening outside.

Sound is another factor; both receiving it and putting it out. The continual hum of city life, combined with planes going overhead, lorries unloading, roadworks and other local noise can drown out a performer. We once had to perform on the south bank of the River Thames, in London, and found it almost impossible to be heard above the background sound of trains, boats, planes and road traffic. At London's Barbican Centre we had to ask for the noisy fountains to be turned off. It is a loss of valuable energy to try to project the voice over the top of such noise and may strain it; so an enclosed space as far away as possible from noise pollution is the ideal situation.

The other side of the coin is the amount of sound you put out. In a square in Manchester our brass band entrée to the show had the telephones of local police stations ringing with complaints because we were surrounded by offices full of people trying to get on with their work. It was a hot day and they had all their windows open. While there are some people who will always complain about street performers (often for obscure ideological reasons), there are obviously genuine causes for complaint; stall-holders can have their business ruined by noise or the crush of crowds watching a show. There may also be other performances happening unavoidably in the same area at the same time. At the Mound in Edinburgh, at festival time the professional street performers get particularly angry at the insensitive use of drumming and electronic amplification. It is best to try to avoid interfering with people's livelihood, especially if they do not share the same passion for street theatre as those who do it.

Related to this is the problem of obstructing a street, particularly in the newly pedestrianised streets of our historic towns, because these tend to be quite narrow. While musicians can play to a passing crowd, an act that requires an audience to stay can completely block the street in a few minutes. People trying to make their way down the street, not seeing the cause of the obstruction, can get frustrated and angry enough to call the police. In a narrow street it is possible for a low-key show to operate with a performing circle as small as a 2-metre radius and to ask the crowd to watch from the sides but, with new people arriving all the time, maintaining this shape requires an inhibiting amount of crowd control.

Another factor to consider when choosing a space is the weather and lighting in general. Night or day, you don't want a strong light behind you, otherwise you will be silhouetted and the audience will be squinting. At night, performing directly under a street light will give a rather ghastly effect. In bright sunlight it is best if the sun is shining from one side because if the performer is squinting all those important eye expressions will be lost. In extremely hot weather shade becomes important. For an energetic show it is usually better if the performer is in shade in order to prevent overheating. Audiences from northern Europe usually like to sit in the sun; further south they are more shade conscious and tend to be very reluctant to come away from it. If it is raining and for some reason you decide to continue with the show it is best to let the audience have whatever shelter there is available. Wind, too, has to be considered. It is surprising how much difference it makes to the carrying of the voice. If a strong wind is blowing sound waves away from the audience, the voice may have to strain to be heard.

The final aspect of location is the physical features in the area. You need to be seen by as many people as possible, so if either you or the audience is raised up, so much the better. The ideal is an amphitheatre situation with the audience on a series of steps and the performer below. This encloses the sound waves and creates a more focused, intimate relationship with the audience. Alternatively, with the performer raised above the audience the voice carries further but loses its volume close by. It also aggrandises the performer by, literally and metaphorically, putting them on a pedestal. Upper levels of all sorts can be useful; sometimes there are rubbish bins or low walls to stand on, even lampposts can be used to leap up if one is agile enough. Avoid too much of a physical barrier, such as a high step or a flower bed, between performer and audience. As stated above, proximity is important; they need to feel that you can physically touch them.

The best way to decide where to play is to put yourself in the audience's position and try to imagine what you will look and sound like there. Is the space conducive to play?

Figure 11 Attracting an audience – will they stop?

ATTRACTING AN AUDIENCE

There are various tactics to gather a crowd and choosing one depends on the nature of the situation. For example, some busking pitches like Covent Garden have an ongoing audience watching one show after another. In this case it is not a problem; simply laying out interesting-looking props is enough to indicate that a show is about to start. Preparing for a show, either by putting on make-up, doing a physical warm-up, or carefully placing props, can be an act in itself. However, this slow build-up is not effective enough either where performers compete for the same crowd, as they do at the Pompidou Centre, or where there is no precedent for a show, such as at a shopping centre.

People going about their ordinary business are hard to divert from their tasks and, although they will notice strange costumes, they will only take much notice either if they are mystified or if they feel they might miss something unique and special. Nowadays there are many charity events that involve fancy dress so it is important to make it immediately clear that you are professional performers. A frequent comment after a show is 'That was very good but what do you do for a living?' It is often assumed that professional performers would not or could not earn their living from street theatre. To dispel these illusions the presentation of a show is important. Amateurs are often betrayed by their lack of care in their costume, so make sure it is attractive and complete. A display of skill or other expertise will give people confidence that they can expect a good show. It is essential to create focus, so performers and musicians who are not engaged in the main action must show the audience where to look by looking at it themselves. This must be maintained throughout the performance.

There are basically two main approaches to attracting an audience; one is to be loud, large and colourful, the other is to be subtle, starting by relating on a one-to-one basis. Both tactics can be used at different stages. The first way is in the tradition of the 'barker' who bawls out a 'Roll up, roll up, ladies an' gen'lemen' speech with useful descriptions of what may follow, plus a few jokes thrown in. Using this method it is important that the barker makes contact with individual members of the public who are closer to hand, as well as reaching those further in the distance. This can create an intimate rapport with those nearby and build the beginnings of solidarity amongst those who have paused to look. Comments about those who choose not to stop sets them apart, an 'us-and-them' situation is created. Loud music, drum rolls and tantalising glimpses of skills and spectacle will add to the desired effect of creating expectation. Mummer & Dada always start with a six-part fanfare played in an acrobatic pyramid; this is not only loud but large, it can be seen and heard from a long way away and is a clear announcement of something exciting about to happen. There is a danger of blasting out too much sound and energy and this will tend to keep people at a distance, or worse – drive some of them away. This is why it is necessary to pitch the energy at varying distances.

The other tactic, relating one-to-one, could use the imitating game, in which people with unusual characteristics walking past are followed and imitated. This may build up a large number of spectators but they will be scattered and so need drawing in to one specific area. Another method is to engage in a simple interaction with one person, such as performing a magic trick for them. This is particularly useful where the passing crowds seem intimidated by performers. People are quite happy to watch someone else being entertained because they are excluded and therefore have no fear of being drawn in or confronted themselves. A small crowd will begin to form quite close up to the centre of attraction. The aim of this tactic is to draw people in by being so low-key that others can't see what is going on from a distance; the sound of laughter or applause from within the crowd creates mystery; other people begin to get curious.

A third possibility exists for large, well-organised groups. At a pre-arranged time all the performers start playing in different places and gradually work their way towards a central location where the main act takes place. Urban Sax manage the difficult feat of doing this while playing brass instruments. The sound can be heard coming from all distant directions and then, as it comes closer and they can hear one another, they co-ordinate the music into one magnificent sound. At Covent Garden they did this by appearing from all sorts of unlikely places including the tops of buildings, slowly descending fire escapes. Another company, the six-person Polish group Snow, place themselves around the area doing eccentric actions which involve a sound; a woman screams, a man walks banging a suitcase on the ground with each step, another has a wind-up air raid siren. They do very little interaction with the crowd – the extremity of their characters makes this difficult – but they traverse the crowd several times, interweaving their sounds into a rhythm, before coming together for their extremely well-acted show. The Natural Theatre Company also use this method with their 'Pink Suitcase' sequence. A group of smart, formally dressed men and women, each with a pink suitcase and an umbrella, spend a frustrating time trying to meet up with each other. When they eventually succeed, the cases are joined together, there is an argument about which way they should go and then they go off together. This tactic has the advantage of combining the freedom and use of the environment that is possible in walkabout theatre with the advantages of the static show.

A further possibility is also useful for walkabout theatre. This is to imitate a real-life situation which would attract attention. For example, the German group Scharlaten Theater imitate a film crew setting up to shoot an advert. It is important to be totally convincing, so they have real cameras which gives them status (and licence to take liberties with people and property). The real ambulance that is used by Trapu Zaharra Teatro Trapero (described in the section on walkabout) instantly attracts a crowd.

In all these cases there is an element of tension or mystery. 'Tension creates attention', as Kevin Brooking so aptly put it. The smashing of bottles, for the purpose of walking and lying upon broken glass, is done slowly and carefully at the Pompidou Centre in order to build a crowd. Loud explosions will immediately turn all eyes but must be followed up by something interesting and more sustainable. The static freeze pioneered by performance artists Gilbert and George in the 1960s, is used today by many mime/robotics performers to arouse initial curiosity. The freeze is not interesting if it is done in a slumped pose but works best if it is held in a position of tension, either midway through an action or in an about-to-do stance. This creation of expectation is a principal factor in holding and increasing the audience.

For the larger groups, advance publicity is the key to attracting an audience but there is sometimes the danger of over-promoting the event. The Urban Sax performance, mentioned above, received considerable press coverage; everyone wanted to be there; it was a marketing success. However, everyone came – the place was so jammed with people that the various trucks and forklifts they had organised to use had no space to move in. Many people could not see and the event was not as spectacular as it could have been. The expected numbers of spectators must be considered well beforehand, especially if the size of the space is limited. It is therefore necessary to examine the different ways to organise the space.

ARRANGING THE AUDIENCE

Once the beginnings of an audience are there the most important thing to do is establish the front row. In southern Europe it is a question of making sure people don't come too far forward. In northern Europe, particularly in Britain where there is such a universal paranoia of being embarrassed in public, it is more difficult for people to be in the front row because of fear of being dragged out and forced to participate. At Covent Garden the ability of performers can be gauged, even before they start, simply by their success in bringing a reluctant audience forward. Children, being less inhibited, are usually quite willing to be directed and don't mind sitting on the ground so much as adults, the problem with them is that they tend to edge forward in the excitement of the show and need a clear demarcation of the performing area. This can be done by carefully placing the audience or even better by something like a rope on the ground. If seating has been arranged make sure that it is placed exactly as you want; it is often a job left to people who aren't aware of the importance of shape and density. Another method of defining the space is the one used by the traditional mummers troupes who would often perform in densely crowded spaces such as pubs. They would process into the space in a long line and pace out a circle while a comic character with a broom would 'sweep' out the people who had been enclosed in the ring.

SHAPE AND SIZE OF THE PERFORMING AREA

The circle is the natural shape for a crowd watching any event. Performing to an audience on every side is possible but not easy. It requires constant turning in order to include the whole circle in what you are doing. Most performers use a three-quarter circle with the equipment and props at the back. This establishes the back and front. The sides are not the best viewing point so if possible it is good to have a slightly elliptical shape with a wide front row and short sides. Other shapes are of course possible. Dogtroep have used a large square shape; triangles are interesting too, but these unnatural shapes have to be clearly defined by barriers otherwise the circle will re-establish. The Spanish group Bekereke have used a long, thin, raised stage with the audience on both sides. It is even possible to have the audience surrounded by the performing area. In this way it is possible for them to watch one scene while another is being prepared behind them.

The size of the performing area will depend not so much on the number of performers, but more on the attractability of the show. On the one hand you want as many people as possible to see the show and this is increased by enlarging the space, on the other hand you don't want it so large that the crowd is either too thin round the edges or too far away for intimate contact and for

Figure 12 The natural circle – slightly elliptical

vocal projection. Sight-lines can be a problem; unless the front rows are sitting down anything that happens low to the ground cannot be seen by anyone more than a few rows back. Amplification and raised stages vastly increase the possible number of spectators but they change the nature of the show completely because they separate the performers and audience.

HOLDING THE AUDIENCE

Many successful shows are quite simply a long build-up to one main act. Even a show with a narrative must have a climax. The build-up must have a pay-off at the end, even if it is not the expected one. For example, an impossibly difficult stunt might be the pretext but it finishes with a comic surprise; Footsbarn announced that their human cannon-ball, Bobby Bullethead, was to be fired through the air and land on an outstretched handkerchief at the back of the crowd. After he was placed in the cannon there was more build-up and misdirection to allow him to leave and run around unnoticed, arriving at the appointed place on cue. A very skilled performer will be able to do something really impressive at the end but, as is the case in other areas of life, the journey is as important as the final destination. Highly skilled jugglers can be uninteresting if they make it look too easy, which is why at circuses there is much building of tension, by means of dimming the lights, drum rolls and several failed attempts before the success. What is essential is to create expectation. Even if the stated aim is clearly impossible, the spectators will wonder how the situation will be resolved; they will not want to walk away from the situation and the more it is built up the bigger the pay-off is expected to be. There is a danger of building up too much expectation if the pay-off is not that wonderful or of taking so long about it that the end result is a disappointment.

This brings us to the most important aspect of performance – timing. Timing cannot be fixed as in a musical score, it has to be gauged according to the mood of the audience. If they are with you then the act can be slowed down and played for all it is worth and more, by improvising, inventing and extending the movements. If they are getting bored or restless, then pace will need to be quickened, but not rushed, otherwise control is lost and it looks desperate.

Another way to create tension, and thereby keep attention, is by interactions with members of the public either as participants or as part of the crowd. Improvisation between performers is often exciting but with volunteers from the audience a different sort of drama is created. The more they are challenged, the more tension is created because the rest of the audience identifies with the volunteer. Therefore, it is important that they come out of the situation well – the audience will feel a collective sense of relief and achievement. These feelings will be the greater the harder the challenge. The danger is going too far so that they become fearful and embarrassed.

Expectation and tension can be built into each section of the show but must also be built into the whole structure. A show with a narrative can set up situations that set the public wondering how they will be resolved. It is less obvious how to create this through-line of expectation in a show consisting of a series of acts without a narrative. One way would be to have equipment, such as a tightrope or fire clubs, which is visible but unused until the end. Another way might be to simply state what the final attraction will be, since it is the visual effect which is the pay-off. Performing artists tend to make less use of this sort of dramatic tension but they make up for it with a love of visual surprises, such as one image emerging from a previous one. Surprise is a key element to any show. It keeps the audience alert and maintains expectation because after one surprise who knows what others might be concealed?

LENGTHS AND ENDS

An outdoor show has been known to last anything from four minutes to four hours. One difference from indoor theatre is that there is often no entrance fee and therefore no expectations as to length. The other major difference is that, if there is no seating, there is a limit as to how long people can stand. They may be prepared to sit on the ground but, if it is wet or dirty, there is no point insisting. Some adults will often take a lot of persuading to sit on the ground at the best of times. If anyone does have to stand they will be reluctant to stay more than forty-five minutes, an hour is possible but not much longer.

The length of a show depends on whether the spectators have arrived with an expectation of seeing it or are being diverted from their pre-planned business. For this reason busking shows are generally very short – an energetic and spectacular break-dancer might do very well with a five-minute sequence. The more frequently the hat is passed the bigger the potential collection. However, most buskers do about half an hour: a twenty-minute show with five minutes each end for setting up and collecting the money. Half an hour is the average length of a 'slot' at Covent Garden. Some buskers work a passing crowd much in the same way as musicians, often not making money rapidly but making up for it by dogged persistence. In Spain I saw a puppeteer-musician keep going for four hours.

Pre-planned theatre shows are able to be longer; usually over half an hour and up to ninety minutes. This allows more scope for building up characters, atmospheres and dramatic situations. There may be organised seating so conventional theatre duration can be used. However, even if there is seating it is not advisable to stretch the show out with an interval; if the spectators have not paid and there are other distractions around they may drift off.

Collecting money or 'bottling' can be done either during the show, or at the end, or both. If it is done continuously during the show it can seem very pushy and is certainly distracting. The best time is just before the end when the climax is about to be reached or just after, before people sense the end coming. The people on the outside of the crowd will have been the last to arrive, so they will be the least involved in the show, the least keen to pay and the first to leave. Ideally, there is someone on the outside of the crowd collecting from these people because the performers can only pass the hat from the centre outwards. Richard Robinson of Covent Garden Community Theatre suggested a good tactic when bottling from the back of the crowd – simply to keep picking coins out of the hat and throwing them back in, accompanied by a 'Thank you. . . . thank you'. This sound suggests to the people watching in front that everyone else is giving very generously and they automatically reach for more coins than they might otherwise have done.

If the performers are experienced they will have found some comic lead-in to the collection. Here is a classic example: after a previous piece of mass participation the audience is introduced to a way to lose weight; first the keep-fit exercises, they must loosen and shake their wrists, wave their arms around, put their hands in their pockets, enclose their money in a fist, pull it out, fold it up, walk several paces forward and put it in the hat. 'You'll lose pounds!' Another familiar line is: 'And now for my last trick I will make half the audience disappear'; the hat is pulled out for the collection and the back row starts to leave. This cleverly brings attention to those people trying to sneak away without paying.

A really successful show doesn't need to employ these tactics. People actually queue up to give you money. In this case it's much better to stay in the centre and let them come to you because in the milling-about the whereabouts of the pecuniary receptacle can be confusing. To help this it is useful to keep some loud patter going. This also lightens the protracted business of collecting. As there is usually no on-site, pre-show advertising it is good policy to make sure all the audience know who you are either by prominently displaying the name or by announcing it at the end – word of mouth is the best publicity.

INTERRUPTIONS

To a good performer most interruptions are not a problem, on the contrary they are a gift. Because they present a situation that could not have been rehearsed, the audience is fascinated to see what will happen and how well it is handled. Solos and duos are much more able to respond than groups unless the group has some pre-arranged action to slip into. Paul Morocco actually encourages interruptions.

Larger groups may be engaged in a theatre piece which involves a 'suspension of disbelief'; everyone pretends the actors are not in the street at all but in their make-believe world. This makes it harder for them to switch out of the reality they have tried so hard to create. However, interruptions must be acknowledged; not doing so suggests insecurity on the part of the actors and it also becomes absurd to try to maintain the illusion if it is being demonstrably undermined. A minor interruption need only be acknowledged by referring to it, but if it threatens to destroy the whole show it is much better for theatre groups to stop pretending, sort it out and then continue. Audiences will give warm sympathetic support if it is well handled. Aggression always looks bad but so does indecisive weakness. The performers must always bear in mind that the audience is there to watch them first so a kind of comic forcefulness is the best policy.

Hecklers should not be a problem, indeed they help to foster the dialogue between performer and audience. Many an inexperienced performer has been saved by a witty heckler. However, some hecklers can be destructive, especially if they are children or drunk, repeating their once funny witticism *ad nauseam*. The best policy in this case is to ignore them (unless you particularly want them to become hysterical). Toddlers will sometimes wander into the performing area. These always upstage anything else that is going on and can get hurt if they are unaware of dangerous flying objects or fast-moving performers. They must be returned to their minders (if you can find them) but be careful to switch into a calmer, quieter gear otherwise they may burst into tears, which prolongs the disruption. If you are able to take the time to have a little interaction with them it can be a winner.

More of a problem are dogs but these too can be a positive advantage. There is a certain type of dog that can be set off by performers; they appear from nowhere, barking incessantly and responding to any advance or retreat as if it was a game. Although this can get a lot of laughs, one has to be careful not to over-excite the dogs otherwise they can become quite vicious. The best policy is to bare your teeth and growl at them. They growl back but with a few sudden advances they are usually overcome and yelp into retreat. It always worked for me, but I suppose it depends on your growl.

Less fun are drunks and other unpredictable people. Street theatre often takes place in areas where there are small groups of people hanging out all day getting intoxicated on one thing or another. In some places they even get territorial about strangers invading 'their' space. Often the interruption will start with some amiable heckling and when volunteers are required they seem suitably uninhibited to be chosen. Only when it is too late do you realise the state that they are in. Sometimes they need no invitation and simply wander into the space. Usually they just want to perform and get a bit of attention, so occasionally it is possible to let them do their bit and they are happy enough to go. The trouble is that usually they don't want to go and it's very difficult to make them. Light-hearted banter almost always fails – they take it that you have included them in the act. If you drop the act and make a genuine entreaty it rarely succeeds, it just makes them more powerful. Anger and aggression must be avoided at all costs – it looks bad and can also lead to a real fight. Gentle, calm physical force has slightly more chance of success, especially if there is a group of you. The best method is to use your powerful position and appeal to the sympathies of the crowd who will be on your side. Get them to shout in unison when fed questions like 'Do you want this intruder on stage?' – 'NO!', or 'Do you want them to go away?' – 'YES!'. With this kind of mass rejection it is hard for them to maintain the illusion that the audience is enjoying their drunken performance and all but the imminently comatose begin to retreat. If they don't appear to be able to get off the ground then another appeal to the audience for strong helpers to extract the fallen angel can have playful possibilities that lighten the heavy air of potential danger.

Police and other uniformed officials can be dealt with by similar methods. They are less of a problem in Britain nowadays but in some countries difficult situations can still arise. The first thing they will do is try to tell you to stop from the edge of the space. When you ignore them and continue (assuming this is what you choose to do), they are obliged to enter the space and approach you. The show has stopped but the spectators will be reluctant to leave, not only because of the real drama unfolding in front of them, but also because they will want to support you. It is possible to use the question-and-answer tactic used for drunks, but this form of mass resistance may not appeal to everyone. It will also raise the level of tension, so that reinforcements are called and you may be arrested for incitement to riot. The best method is to leave the space, join the audience and lead them in ironic applause and cheers. This puts the police in the position of performer and draws attention to the fact that the uniform is only a costume and they are only acting the tough authoritarian role. Usually they can't quite cope with this and begin to edge out of the area; you can then return to more applause and attempt to finish the show before reinforcements arrive.

Rain is another serious disruption, particularly showers. If there is a steady downpour there is no point in attempting to do a show, but if there are showers it is hard to know whether to risk setting up the gear and whether an audience will materialise. In this case, the shorter the show and the lighter the equipment, the better. Once the audience has been assembled and the show has begun, it is best to ignore light rain until the audience starts to become disheartened. In general, the rule is to keep going as long as the audience stays, unless the act becomes dangerous when slippery. However, an experienced audience (such as would be found at a street theatre festival like Limburg) is often well enough prepared, so that the onset of rain is followed by a rustling of waterproofs and a ruffling of umbrellas. This leaves the audience happy enough but the poor performers get drenched. Shows can be stopped and restarted later with surprising ease if the audience has the time to wait.

Other frequent disruptions are vehicles trying to get through the crowd, the sound of planes or sirens making it impossible to be heard, or the distraction caused by other shows. In all these cases the show may have to be stopped and, if possible, restarted. There is no point in getting frustrated or depressed, there is nothing to be done – it is in the nature of street theatre and anyway all can be used to your advantage if you are prepared to change the nature of the game.

COSTUMES, PROPS AND SET

The nature and style of costumes, props and set will obviously be dictated mainly by the requirements of each particular show. However, there are a few general considerations for their use in outdoor theatre.

Outdoors, the environment, whether it is a park, street, or field, will be a very dominant factor. Whereas many walkabout performers choose to blend in with the environment (for reasons discussed later), most performers involved in stationary shows need to stand out from the crowd. Even if a naturalistic appearance is used, a slight exaggeration of certain subtle features makes them more watchable. In any case a group will need to be unified by the style of their costumes. In order to stand out well, it is best to be bold in both colour and design. Some groups have a completely non-naturalistic style so they use one main colour for the whole group – Malabar and Forkbeard use all red, Generik Vapeur used bright blue. Two contrasting colours work well – Boîte à Pandore use grey and yellow and Dogtroep have their wonderful black and white mottled costumes. Streets are dirty places so light colours are not always the most practical.

Changing costume can be a problem for small-scale shows that do not have any sort of set. Performers may not mind stripping off, but it can be quite a distraction if the focus is supposed to be elsewhere. It is best to under-dress and peel off an outside layer because putting on clothes takes longer and is more painstaking. Stripping off can be an act in itself, revealing the second costume at its best, rather than limp and empty. Buskers have to be ready to do their shows at short notice and therefore either under-dress or use a costume which is not so uncomfortable or eccentric that they cannot walk round in it for the rest of the day. For the same reason make-up, if used at all, tends to be quite basic, unless the process of making up is used to attract an audience. On the other hand, theatre groups, particularly the performing artists, sometimes use a very bold make-up, such as a bright blue or red, over all exposed skin areas, to fit in with the bold costumes. Welfare State used black and white stripes down

the face until they realised that this created a mask which distanced the performer from the spectators.

The main practical consideration for props, sets and costume
is that of mobility. The more equipment that has to be transported, the more limited the performer is, in terms of choosing
where and when to play. The busker often operates without a
vehicle, so everything must be carried in one or two bags. At the
end of the day the performers will also have to carry the weight
of coins. Even if a vehicle is used, life can be made much easier
by trolleys such as the ones used by Boîte à Pandore. Even
supermarket trolleys can be used although their wheels are too
small to cope with gravel paths and uneven surfaces. Supermarket trolleys are also an awkward shape to pack away inside a
vehicle. Some groups, such as Metafolis, use a trailer towed
behind the vehicle to add to capacity. The only trouble with
these is that they are rather easily stolen, so it is best not to put
the most expensive equipment inside them. The set-up of
Metafolis is extremely efficient. They carry sheets of corrugated
iron which are an effective backdrop. These are surprisingly
light to handle and are easily stowed on the top of their large
van. They are easily bolted together and strong enough to be
wind resistant, especially when they are connected to the vehicle
itself. The group use the top of the van as a performance/music
area so that the equipment is safe from thieving fingers. They
use the stability and bulk of the vehicle to attach their amazing
rotating device.

Some British theatre and community groups have converted
double-decker buses into performance/accommodation facilities. The Scottish group Clown Jewels tour with three of them,
to which various contraptions such as trapeze and inflatables are
attached. Perhaps the most elaborate conversion was the bus
used by Stage Space and later by Snowball. This had a whole
stage hinged on to one side of it, which could be lowered to a
horizontal position and rested on hinged legs. This revealed the
set, which had three levels – the stage, the upper deck and the
roof, which had other removable additions built on to it. The
problem with such large vehicles is manoeuvring in and out of
narrow streets, through field gates and round tight corners;
towns, at festival time, are often decorated with bunting across
the streets which makes access to the centre of activity completely impossible for something as tall as a double-decker bus.

There is a natural desire to expand but having encountered endless logistical problems such as these, it is with envy that some groups look at much simpler arrangements. There is the Smallest Theatre in the World, a side-car of a motor cycle, inside which a single performer re-creates Shakespearean plays to a total audience of one. Also, there is the ingenious arrangement of the American juggler Narbo, who lives in Paris. He transports an entire little circus in his suitcase. He has a set of lightweight flat boards, about 0.5 metre long, that are riveted together so that they fold out to form one long strip. This is bent round into a circle and held vertical by pairs of shelf brackets attached to small strips of wood. These act as ring boards, defining the space very neatly and giving the space a colourful frame so that the area within feels more special. He also has a small, free-standing, lightweight tent, closed on all sides, which acts as a backdrop, as a changing room and to conceal surprises. It needs to be free-standing and very stable to avoid pegging into the ground and to avoid carrying weights. Wind can be a major problem for all large, flat surfaces. The normal indoor theatre flats are quite impractical for this reason. If a backdrop is required it will be better if it hangs loose so that a breeze does not push it over. Slits in the cloth let wind pass through; narrow strips of cloth are even better. Mummer & Dada used their costume rail as a backdrop thus serving a dual purpose.

In the same way the effect of props has to be balanced against their transportability – it is no good having a 6-foot dragon for a two-minute sequence, especially if it does not dismantle for packing away. For this reason it is best if props have a number of functions. Neutral objects such as pieces of cloth, poles and boxes can be used in many different ways to make costume, set and props and they can easily pack away. On the other hand objects such as footballs, although light, take up a lot of space and unless they are used extensively are a trouble to pack. (They also seem to roll or get kicked away rather frequently.) Hats are better if they are soft or squashable (like the old opera-type top hats), otherwise they begin to look battered very quickly.

Large masks also take up a lot of space unless they can fit inside each other or be filled. There is very little mask work done outside, which is surprising considering the large number of mime/robotics experts and the historical precedent of the commedia dell'arte. Large, full-face masks combined with large gestures work well at long distance. Half-face masks only work well at a fairly short distance because the mouth and eyes need to be seen in order to animate the mask. Also, because they reveal more of the personality of the performer they need to be seen closer to make the most of the contact with the audience.

As can be seen, the size of the operation is a major factor in determining the type of equipment that can be used. To explore the nature of different-sized static shows it is necessary to break them down into three groups: solos and duos; small-scale groups; and large-scale theatre.

Chapter 9

Solos and duos

The majority of street performers work on their own. This is usually because the money is better. The amount of income for each show, whether through money into the hat or by pre-arranged fee, varies according to length and quality rather than by the number of performers. So some solo shows can make a lot of money whereas most groups find it hard to survive without other support. A solo who is considering performing with someone else has to bear in mind that this will mean halving their income.

The solo has total control of the show. The relationship is simply between him or her and the audience (although a solo can also relate to objects). This means that there tends to be more contact with the audience – everything must be directed towards the audience because there is no one else to relate to. It also allows for greater flexibility and spontaneity. The solo is free to drop the usual routine and go off in a completely improvised direction. However, it is a very lonely existence – no one to share those extremes of success and failure and no one to spark off. So solos are often interested in experimenting with working with other people; the trouble is that, being used to having total control, they are reluctant to let go of it.

Good long-standing duos are quite rare but quite special. The single performer/audience relationship of the solo is quad-rupled; there is the relationship of the combined duo relating to the audience, the relationship between the partners and finally the two individual relationships with the audience; for example, if one is high status he or she would look down their nose at the audience, if the other is low status he or she would be obse-quious. The advantage of duos is that, assuming they have built

up a good improvisational rapport, they can retain the flexibility
of the solo while enormously increasing their possibilities. With a
trio the possibilities are further increased but it is much harder
to co-ordinate spontaneous reactions, therefore there is an
increased danger of working against each other unless, of
course, they are experienced specialists in improvisation.

Solos and duos are quite vulnerable. They can be crowded out
by bigger shows or have difficulty in dominating the environment. For this reason they tend to do large things like ride 10-
foot unicycles, blow fire, walk a tightrope, or juggle high into the
air. There are other ways to be large – by being extreme, like the
provocateurs Chris Lynham and Leo Bassi, or by getting other
people involved as do the animators. Dominating large spaces,
such as those at Covent Garden and the Pompidou Centre, can
be very exhausting so, although solos and duos can have a liberty
and financial success unavailable to performers in groups, they
have to pay for it in other ways.

PAUL MOROCCO: THE VITAL ART OF ENTERTAINING

Paul Morocco is an American performer based in Britain who
has succeeded in taking a fairly straightforward (although
highly skilled) juggling show into the realms of high-class street
theatre. He has some original versions of the usual routines –
juggling fruit, such as large and heavy melons, which he throws
higher and higher until catastrophe happens. However, it is not
the skills that make him special. It is his openness to whatever
happens that warms the public and keeps the show fresh and
alive.

In the streets there are sometimes people who have a negative
attitude towards street theatre; perhaps it obstructs their passage
or they disapprove of it. Sometimes they take a destructive
macho attitude – some upstart foreign juggler is in their street
and they have to prove that they are not frightened of walking
through his space. Paul uses and even encourages these interruptions by coming so far away from his back wall that the
performing area blocks much of the street and the line of the
audience at the back is thin enough to penetrate easily. Each
time somebody crosses the space, Paul leaves the presentation of
the tricks to rush back and get into some sort of interaction with
the intruders. He may follow and imitate them or playfully get

in their way, as if not knowing which way to get past them. He may go into a quick on-the-spot interview with them – what do they think of the show, of politicians, of the quality of the shops, etc. He may even offer a service such as carrying their shopping bags from one side of the space to the other. He imitates and exaggerates their reaction to him, whether it is giggling, aggression, or indifference. It is the risks he takes that give the show a real edge of danger as he confronts these people; he is not intimidated by big, aggressive men or by high-status, strait-laced people or even by police. He tries to draw them all into his game.

This is the real theme of the show. He draws attention to people's refusal to relax and have fun and, by doing so, ridicules the attitude they hold towards him. This is not done in an aggressive or smart-arsed way, such an attitude would hardly warm the audience, but it is clear that it is not the individuals he is making fun of, so much as the curious problem they have in being open to a moment of play. There is an element of the court jester in this confrontation between the stony faces of the sensible and serious and the frivolous frolics of the funny man. Indeed, like the court jester, there is a very real risk of being punched, arrested, or abused for drawing attention to the truth of the situation. The reason he does not seem to be making himself look clever at other people's expense is that he is quite willing to make fun of himself and is not afraid of failing or being exposed. If it goes wrong he plays the failure fully, being exaggeratedly apologetic to the person concerned and to the audience.

All the gestures, emotions and exaggerated postures are done at a high level of energy and alertness. Because the show is largely improvised, the audience is witnessing a person in a state of heightened vitality, alert, skilful, living 100 per cent in the moment, letting the events flow through him and not forcing the situation. It is this state of 'being' that is so entrancing for the audience.

KEVIN BROOKING: WHY DID HE CROSS THE ROAD?

A ragged tramp stands on the corner of the street. He shivers, even though it is a warm summer's day, for him it is always winter. Beside him is a strange-looking cart – a toboggan with different-sized wheels supports an old-fashioned wooden radio,

Figure 13 Kevin Brooking makes contact with the traffic

complete with aerial, a trumpet, a wicker basket and a bunch of carrots. Attached to the wheels is a series of cogs which rotate a cylindrical toy. This emits the sound of a sheep when it is inverted, so that the cart 'baas' as it moves along.

Pulling this contraption, he walks down the street with short, flat-footed steps, the semi-detached soles of his shoes slopping on his feet. Under his arm are eight aluminium tent poles. Passers-by give him curious, slightly fearful glances. He waits patiently while trying to cross a busy one-way street until a car stops to let him cross, but at that moment he appears not to notice this kindness; he is blankly staring into the space ahead of him, the earflaps of his hat blinkering his vision. The car hoots to attract his attention and he jumps with fright, much to the amusement of a few onlookers who have stopped to watch this strange figure. A series of miscomprehended signals as to whether he is letting the car go first leads to a near collision. He is waved across but misunderstands the waving and so waves back. After more gesticulations he pulls out a metal funnel with a rubber glove attached over the wide end. When he blows down the narrow end the glove inflates, waving back; he sucks and it suddenly disappears. After all, he sets out across the street but half-way across he drops an aluminium pole. He picks it up but drops another and this continues until he completes the disaster by dropping them all. He shrugs an apology to the patient driver whose amusement gets the better of his irritation. The number of onlookers grows, as does the queue of cars behind.

Having recovered all the tubes, he tries to make up for the delay by polishing the lights of the car, then the windscreen, then the bonnet, and ends up by holding a handstand on the bonnet. The driver cannot resist the temptation to put him off-balance by lurching the car forward. Kevin exaggerates the collapse and having succeeded in engaging the driver in a game, he plays being annoyed with the driver. The number of specta-tors grows. Meanwhile the drivers of the cars behind, unable to see the cause of the obstruction, are becoming frustrated. The hooting of car horns starts to build up. Kevin pulls out his trumpet and, having established enough rapport with the first car to be permitted to handstand on the car, he stands on the bonnet and honks back. This increases the volume of hooting from all the way back down the street. When he has got them all going, he stands on the roof of the car and plays the well-known, end-of-comic-routine musical phrase which ends with two notes. He plays the first part of the phrase and, producing one of his tubes, he conducts the response, repeating the exercise until he has achieved a chorus of horns that is in time enough to suit him. He bows like a great conductor, getting a huge round of applause from the crowd, leaps off the car and returns to his little cart, where he ignites a couple of small fireworks that shoot out the back like jet propulsion, and completes his passage across the street. This incident was a spontaneous improvisation on the way to do his show inside a small park.

Kevin Brooking is an American performer, based in Brussels, whose background is American circus and training at Lecoq's school. His extensive circus skills are complemented by his quirky inventiveness and an ability to create a warm, gentle play. Few other performers could have succeeded in charming a busy street to such an extent. It takes courage to delay traffic and risk the drivers' anger. It takes even more delicacy to induce a line of frustrated car drivers into playing a game. As can be seen, he starts off by establishing a rapport with one or two people, taking a few liberties but using extreme care that no damage can be done. For example, he wears rubber-soled shoes that won't scratch paintwork, he tests the strength of the car before putting his full weight on it and in the same way he tests the flexibility of his playmates before imposing on them. He reassures them, indirectly, by the prepared skills and surprises that he is able to draw upon. Most of all, he demonstrates that he wants to give everyone a good time so they do not need to fear his imposition. The naivety and harmlessness of his clown character makes it hard for members of the public to be too tough with him – they would only be making bigger fools of themselves. Like a playful dog which keeps bringing back a stick, he makes a simple demand that is hard to refuse – a demand that they try, for a moment, to forget their desire to be somewhere else and enjoy where they are. Why did Kevin Brooking cross the road? It was certainly not just to get to the other side.

Chapter 10

Small-scale groups

Small-scale groups are those of under ten people, usually only about four or five. The technical possibilities with this number of people are much greater; a bigger set can be erected for each performance but more importantly some members can hold the attention while others are engaged in other things. This could be supporting the main action with live music or visual effects, or preparing for the next sequence. For example, costumes can be changed, which gives an almost unlimited number of characters. This means that a story-line is possible; many groups of this size contain actors who would call their work 'theatre' rather than performers doing shows. Having more people also shares the responsibility for the success and failure of the show, which can reduce stress on one level. However, the internal organisation necessary for the required co-operation can raise other areas of stress.

The logistics of groups are quite different from solos and duos. Since busking is not really a viable option (without other means of support) groups will usually be paid by a pre-arranged fee or by ticket sales. This introduces a host of other consequences. It means that they will have to play at pre-arranged times, thus losing the liberty enjoyed by solos. It also means that certain expectations of quality must be fulfilled – a guaranteed, repeatable product; which in turn means that fewer risks can be taken. Risks are made even more difficult by the complexity of relationships within the group. If a departure from what has been rehearsed is too radical and unexpected it may leave others in a very difficult situation. This lack of flexibility reduces the amount of interaction with the audience. The actors will be too preoccupied with the interplay between each other to allow much room for another dimension. This turns the show inwards even though much may still be directed outwards.

The nature of the creative process is quite different for groups. A solo can change his or her act each time he or she does it. A group needs to agree and communicate all the changes, so there has to be a much more thorough rehearsal time. The complexities mean there will have to be much more of an organisational structure, either co-operatively or under the guidance of leaders. Because so much has to be pre-arranged the emphasis is more on controlled sequences rather than on energy and inspired play.

Groups obviously need a larger area to play in than one or two people. A performing space 4 or 5 metres across would be quite cramped for five people. This means that there is less choice of location; streets become less appropriate. However, they will be able to dominate large spaces, even with other events happening, when smaller shows would get squeezed out. Groups need a minimum of thirty people in the audience otherwise they begin to look ludicrous. The maximum number could be anything up to 6,000, depending on the acoustics of the place. More than this, and the distance between the back row of the audience and the performers would necessitate amplification and/or large structures of the sort discussed in the next section. Smaller groups would be rather overstretched for this type of operation. Small groups may lose out on interplay with the audience but they still maintain a human dimension. Intimacy and immediacy are used to their full advantage. They tend not to use amplification so the vocal and other abilities of the performer are central to the performance. On an even larger scale these factors begin to get lost.

MUMMER & DADA GO TO HELL (AND BACK)

Mummer & Dada is a company I founded, performed with and later directed. Although it is hard to be objective about one's own work it is important to give a brief description of our work, not only because it has helped to formulate many of the ideas within this book, but also because the group has an unusual crossover between the worlds of busking, circus and the more consciously artistic theatre.

We are a group of six performers of different nationalities,

French, Brazilian and American as well as English. We are based
in Bristol and started up in 1985 with a combination of ex-Lecoq
students and members of Kaboodle. Kaboodle had developed
the idea of circus theatre in the late 1970s and we have taken it a
stage further. Originally Mummer & Dada was thought of as a
collaboration between performers who had already developed
their own work. Within a few years this loose association of solos
had merged into a group with its own style and hierarchy. In our
first year we presented a simple twenty-minute piece based on
the mummers' plays. This established a style which we continued
to develop over the years. This incorporated direct contact with
the audience, the death and resurrection theme and an interest
in Dada which led us to try juxtaposing an odd mix of skills,
styles and images. This mix is helped by the diverse cultural
backgrounds within the group. We are part entertainers, part
communicators, with an element of performing artist.

We made a new show every year, gradually increasing the
length of the piece up to the one and a half hours of 'Fools Gold'
in 1990. The expansion was not only in terms of time but also in
the amount of equipment we took with us. In the first year a
supermarket trolley was big enough to contain all the props and
instruments; by 1990 we needed two large vehicles to carry
sound equipment, a set capable of supporting various trapeze
gear, and masks and costumes for three different types of show
– a procession, a cabaret and the main theatre show. The types
of venue also changed over the years – originally the same show
was used in a whole range of outdoor spaces, in 1989 we toured
with a marquee and by 1990 were doing about a third of our
shows inside theatres.

The extent of this move into indoor theatre is quite unusual
and was brought about by our frustration with the conditions
and status of performing outdoors. In the early years we were
also very unusual for having so many performers in a show that
earned a substantial amount of its income through busking.
Attempting to have a narrative is also uncommon at that level,
just possible for short shows – the time-length could be
increased the more we moved away from the limitations of
busking.

Our aim is to create a theatre that has universal appeal, that
works as a simple entertainment as well as on a more artistically
sophisticated and meaningful level. Circus skills provided a

useful link between popular culture and avant-garde physical theatre. We use themes which have a specific political relevance (such as dealing with self-righteousness during the Thatcher years) as well as a general humanistic one. Since society has become so fractured into sub-cultures, it is necessary to use stories and archetypes that transcend divisions of age, sex and class. In so doing, it is also possible to transcend differences between national cultures. For example, in the year that we were planning to tour in Brazil, Ireland and the continent of Europe, we used a great deal of Catholic imagery. By also using a story based on Greek myth, we tapped into the common European cultural heritage so that the story was not unfamiliar whatever country we went to. The advantage of using familiar stories or characters is that they give secure markers for a public which is unused to theatre. There is also a great deal of background knowledge that only needs to be implied, so that the interpretation of the cliché becomes a statement. These archetypes are not only to be found in the past but in the contemporary culture. We have used King Kong and Superman as well as figures like Robin Hood.

We took the mummers' plays as a pattern because they work on many different levels – that of simple entertainment, of charming amateur dramatics, and of myth. The basic scenario of challenge, conflict, death and life renewal has much scope for different sorts of treatment. Another reason is because we were interested in a juxtaposition and interaction of different nationalities and so we used a tradition that represents one of the last living vestiges of English folk culture. A tradition that predates Christianity and the less appealing overlay of jingoistic British culture.

Once the style became established, so did a working method. Normally, I would produce a simple scenario, with a rough idea of which routines would be used and where they should be placed. About half our rehearsal time would be used working on acrobatic, juggling and music techniques and trying to see how they could be used dramatically. The other half of the time would be spent experimenting with objects, improvising and working on comic routines to fill out the rest of the story. There was very little discussion as time was usually very limited: one year we devised two shows (about ninety minutes of fairly tight routines) in two and a half weeks. The performers were encouraged to make the most of their parts so, inevitably, the show became embellished by words and action during the course of the tour; a spontaneous improvisation in one show would become adopted as a permanent feature and less inspired material would be pruned out.

Probably the most successful show in recent years was 'Hell Is Not So Hot', which broke with the unity of time, place and action that was part of the mummers' tradition and had been used up to that point. Creating scenes set in different places is more difficult outdoors because the environment is such an intrusive and dominant factor. This was not just a simple change of place either, but a whole journey, following the path of a hero who searches for his lost lover in the regions of the dead. He crosses the River Styx, goes to Heaven, Purgatory and Hell. Here, there is a revolution and finally a battle between angels and devils which is resolved when God appears. The change of scenes was aided by the use of a large, blue cloth, attached to poles, which became a boat, a river, a ghostly shroud and finally God's costume. Numerous circus skills were integrated into the theatre: for example, there was a sequence with angels juggling fifteen halos, an acrobatic fight, stunts such as knife-throwing, lying on a bed of nails and walking on broken glass as the tortures of Hell, an escapology trick as the heroine broke free from her chains and various magic tricks interspersed throughout the piece. Masks were also used to good effect, particularly animal masks – an entire fish on an actor's head looked like something from a painting by Chagall; dog masks were used for the three heads of Cerberus; and a large chicken made a brief appearance, Dada like, for no apparent reason whatsoever.

Perhaps the scene that best encapsulated the style of the show was the first sequence in which the actors disputed at what point to start the story and ended up by going all the way back to the beginning of time – the creation of the universe. God stood on a box, narrating and orchestrating the events while the others created the images. The Big Bang was a pyrotechnic device which failed to go off and then unexpectedly did so; the planets hurtling in all directions was a co-ordinated chaos of juggling balls, clubs, rings, spinning plates and a plastic pineapple, whooshed around the space. The genesis of life was shown by the actors presenting themselves as chemical elements, each with a flat stick, with which they jigged a morris dance, forming the traditional interwoven star, which was announced to be the first cell. Early life-forms were shown by an arrangement of bodies to form the shape of a dinosaur. Apes were presented in the cliché of the three monkeys who hear no evil, see no evil, speak no evil and a fourth who closed another orifice. The impossibility of portraying such an epic panorama of events made the attempt more naive and charming. The contrast between image and method made good comedy as well as introducing the imaginative leap required. It also juxtaposed an odd mix of techniques and visual surprises which set the tone for the rest of the piece.

However, judging from the comments we received, it was the performances that stood out as much as the skills and effects. The strength of the piece was that it operated on two levels – the group of actors who argued, interrupted and commented on the play, and the narrative itself. The characters of the actors were extensions of the personalities of the performers themselves. This meant that dropping out of character, either to improvise, comment on the play, or deal with an interruption, could be done within the context of the piece. The ability to switch from being inside the narrative to being actors maintained a light-hearted level of 'alienation' and also solved the problem of enclosing the drama within the piece to the exclusion of the audience. Emotional scenes could be played for real and then made fun of. This device is not new, it was pioneered by Brecht in the 1930s, but it is very suited to the honesty of the street situation; there is an ongoing self-parody. The problem is to avoid parodying so much that the narrative is destroyed. For this reason it is important that the actors enjoy their role in the narrative and play it fully – only afterwards can it be made fun of. This balance between the basic level of street performing and more theatrical/artistic methods is hard to maintain because it requires actors who are experienced in both areas and that, at least in Britain, is quite rare.

LA FUERA DELS BAUS PERFORM 'ACCIONS'

The FDB, which comes from Catalonia, experiments with and investigates cultural aspects in the search for new forms of expressions and ways of dealing with the public. . . . The FDB is not a social phenomenon; it is not a group; it is not a circle of friends; it is not an association in favour of anything. FDB is a subversive organisation within the theatre's present panorama.

(from the publicity for 'Accions', Lisbon, 1987)

The show 'Accions' stunned audiences when the Fuera dels Baus (FDB) presented it at the festival of new theatre and dance in Lisbon in 1987. They described it as 'the alteration of a concrete space, a game without rules, a slap in the face. We are not sure that the spectator will go out the same person he came in as, but we guarantee our sound explosions, our shock tactics.'

The show was scheduled to be shown at an outdoor amphitheatre next to the Gulbenkian Art Museum. It was part of a two-week theatre festival which attracted the cultural elite of Lisbon. Since they knew the theatre and since there were no seat numbers on the tickets, everyone arrived early to get a good seat. However, there was a long delay, possibly deliberate, which raised the level of excitement and pressure around the entrance gate to claustrophobic proportions. Finally, at least half an hour after the scheduled starting time, the gates were opened and the crowd surged in. When they arrived at the amphitheatre, however, the seats had been covered with tarpaulins to prevent anyone sitting there. The already disgruntled audience now became thoroughly confused, there was nowhere to go but on to the stage area where they inspected the 'set', which consisted of an old car and a huge, white, plastic sheet strung up vertically, with a criss-cross of ropes in front of it. They carefully assessed these objects as if they were in an art gallery.

A rock band came on to a side stage and began to play powerful music, very loudly, which continued throughout the rest of the performance. Most of the spectators did not like the music but condescended to maintain a distanced interest in the phenomenon. All of a sudden there was a loud explosion from the top of a scaffolding tower and a wall of concrete blocks, behind the seating, began to be demolished by two men in suits and dark glasses. One had a sledge-hammer, the other a long-handled axe. Bursts of flame lit the scene. Having knocked down a big enough hole for them to get through, they emerged screaming, crawling over the covered seats and menacing the audience. They swung their tools, clearing a way through the spectators, and began to smash up the car and then hack it to pieces. When sections, such as a door, came loose, they hurled them at the audience, breaking up the settled circle that had formed around the car. They energetically hacked down the centre of the roof and then prised it apart, before dismembering it from the rest of the body. Eventually only the chassis and the engine were left with bits of twisted metal littering the stage.

The frenetic music transformed to a more melancholic drone. From high up in the falling darkness a naked, whitened man was spotlighted in blue, suspended from a cable which slanted between the tower and the opposite side of the stage. The figure slowly descended across the heads of the audience, followed by another naked figure, a woman. They were suspended by a harness so that they hung horizontally, free to move their arms and legs with slow extended movements, half flying, half writhing. Strapped to their bodies were bags of liquid which dripped so that the image had a beautiful, elemental, embryonic quality. Other naked figures emerged at the side of the stage, as if from out of the ground. These moved as if frail from starvation, they staggered towards members of the public, their eyes pleading. The two suited characters returned and threw large quantities of brightly coloured paint at them. The audience had to scatter again to avoid being splashed with colour, but because there were now about six naked figures in the area, retreating in all directions, there was much confusion and many of the spectators found themselves tainted. In order to avoid the paint it was necessary to stay away from the naked figures but they continued to approach, gesturing for help. Covered in different colours, they retreated up on to the network of ropes, their bodies creating an extraordinary, multi-coloured pattern on the white screen. The two suited characters pulled a couple of fire-hoses on to the stage and, poised like machine-gunners, used them as water cannon. The force of the jets thrust the figures against the sheet, washing the paint off them and streaking the paint on the sheet. Gradually the figures collapsed, hanging off the ropes, limp and Christ-like, until they became a tangled mass of bleached, dead bodies on the ground.

The company challenged the audience's conception of theatre. Many of the fur-coated bourgeoisie did not appreciate the joke of the covered seats. They were shocked by the violence and the apparent disregard for the sensibilities and safety of the audience. Worst of all, the performers had threatened to get paint on the spectators' modish theatre wear. In another show some of the actors ripped up raw meat and ate it. Of course, many of the audience were offended and would refuse to go and see anything like it again. There are people who refuse to acknowledge the unpleasant aspects of the modern world and the company, in this show, sought to draw attention to subjects like Third World hunger, oppression, urban frustration and the anger at everything that is represented by the motor car. The uncompromising dynamic of their work appeals especially to urban youth. They have influenced many other groups including the French 'rock theatre' groups, such as Malabar and Archaos, that draw their energy from the revolutionary anger and love of anarchy, which comes out of the bleak wastelands of the high-rise suburbs.

It is important to note that the violence directed out towards the audience is carefully controlled. The actor throwing the car door lifted it high in the air, threatening, but also pausing that one second before aiming it at a reasonably safe area. The skill lies in playing right at the borderline of safety without harming people. Occasionally accidents happen but if it looks too safe the whole effect is lost. In northern Europe we play within very safe boundaries but southern Europeans, with their taste for carnival, appreciate the exhilaration of danger.

Chapter 11

Large-scale theatre

Audience numbers for large-scale theatre work can vary enormously; from a few thousand up to the 15,000 who watched Welfare State's 'Burning of the Houses of Parliament' in 1981. Without the aid of an amphitheatre it is hard to imagine many more being able to see a single event. Welfare State were helped by their choice of location on top of a hill.

On this kind of scale, many of the audience will be at least a hundred yards away from the performers; at this distance facial expression becomes indistinguishable and the unamplified voice will be inaudible. The human scale is reduced. In a rock concert, vocal and facial expression are essential to satisfy the expectations of the audience, so modern technology in the form of amplification and huge video screens is needed to reduce the effect of distance. Although facial expression cannot be seen unaided, whole body movements can be, especially if they are multiplicated by others onstage. For this reason mass choreography is another technique used in big spectacles. The British experimental group Lumiere & Son have developed this aspect in their outdoor performances. Another way to amplify human body expression is by using stilts.

Because of the distance, large images are needed to replace the reduced immediacy of the human scale. These images might be in the form of the set or large puppets, inflatables, or firework displays. These are all techniques that are used at rock concerts and at huge outdoor events such as the opening of the Olympic Games. The theatricalisation of these types of event makes it hard to distinguish between theatre and pure spectacle. It is not the purpose of this book to go into too theoretical a discussion about what is theatre but it is important to note that there is a difference between the mere use of spectacular effects and their use in a dramatic way. Choreographing large numbers of people on and off stage can be very impressive in itself. Military parades are a demonstration of organisational ability, discipline and, by implication, power. However, if it is to be more than a display of the director's megalomania, it is important that the dramatic effect is well used. Similarly, stage effects and pyrotechnics must be used carefully. Theatrical effects have been seducing audiences since the early days of stage machinery but when the effects start to dominate the human scale there is a danger of the human drama being lost. We can be impressed by effects, but we need to be involved in a drama in order for the theatrical experience to take place. Choreographing hundreds of people and setting off thousands of pounds' worth of fireworks can be surprisingly disappointing if they are not part of a drama. Welfare State understand this very well, their fireworks at the end of 'The Burning of the Houses of Parliament' expressed the exhilaration of revolution. Royal de Luxe use spectacular pyrotechnics to simulate the battlefields of the First World War.

The artistic problem of large-scale theatre is how to maintain a drama with the human scale dominated by these huge effects. There is no point in going into subtle subplots or even deeply rounded characterisation. A simple conflict with a resolution is needed. Welfare State frequently use revolution as a theme; the Inflatable Theatre Company have St George battling with a vast inflatable dragon. Within these simple themes there is some room for fine detail but it is size and surprise which really count. Malabar's show 'Face à Face', is a good example of this. It consists of a sci-fi battle between white moth-like creatures on high stilts and a tribe of red and black punks with motor bikes and chains and an armoured van with a rock band mounted on the top. The basic conflict is made more interesting by the reversals of fortune – prisoners captured, rescues, exchange of hostages, individual acts of daring and an apocalyptic climax. The battle is waged by means of pyrotechnics and circus skills. The emphasis is on powerful spectacle rather than subtle atmosphere.

Les Sharpe of Emergency Exit summarised the need for simplicity:

If working on a large scale, there are not the same opportunities for explanatory text, sequential and literal plots. They are inappropriate on this scale. Visuals are more immediate, they have more resonance, like music. One of the mistakes we have sometimes made is to become over-complicated and, although you may think it is simple, the audience cannot make head or tail of it. The story should be simple enough to explain in one or two sentences so that what you do to get from A to B can be much richer.

There are two ways these large shows can be organised. The first way is as a one-off piece commissioned for a specific event; these are usually site-specific and will be dealt with in the next chapter. The second way is as a repeatable product touring in much the same way as a smaller group. The increased scale means a greater emphasis on technical effects and therefore there will be a much higher ratio of technicians to performers. It is usually too expensive to tour with a huge cast so mass choreography tends to be restricted to the site-specific event. Nevertheless there needs to be a large team on tour (from thirty to fifty). These travel much in the same way as a circus, with their own mobile homes, because this will be cheaper than hotels over a long tour. It is also preferred because of the need to be able to retreat to personal privacy.

The size of the shows makes it difficult to exclude a non-paying audience so normally they are paid for either by local councils or a festival or both. Because of this they generally have to appeal to an even wider audience than might stop and watch a show in the street. This means that they have to be careful about being too artistically avant-garde. Not only do they have to cater for a wide range of tastes but they must be careful about offending people in other ways. Local people may be very suspicious of this invasion of vehicles and they may not like having their lives disturbed. Generik Vapeur decided to schedule one of their shows at the unusual hour of breakfast time. The deafening loud bangs brought bleary-eyed residents to their windows with some gestures of evident disapproval.

Sight-lines can be a problem for this size of show. Royal de Luxe arrange for grandstand-type seating to be erected. This can be hugely expensive. Malabar have no seating provided, so they raise performers up on vehicles and stilts. If a crowd cannot see well it can become very frustrated and if there are no barriers or stewards the situation may turn very dangerous. A location may be found that has good sight-lines and other positive advantages; however, on this scale, there may not be a lot of choice and the group will be forced to play somewhere quite unsuitable. For this reason active co-operation with local authorities is essential. (This subject is covered by the interview with Robin Morley in the next section.) Bureaucratic attitudes vary from country to country. When IOU performed near a railway yard in Copenhagen they were able to use the unusual spectacle of moving railway trucks as part of the show. Enquiring about repeating this in England they were told; 'Oh no, we can't let that happen. If we let you do it they'll all be at it'; as if there would suddenly be scores of theatre groups queuing up to play with their trains.

Once the show is set up, the running of it needs to be very carefully considered. With the group spread out in different parts of the area, they may need to be organised in teams linked by short-wave radio to a central control, which gives the all-important timing. Co-ordination and technical mastery are essential. With so much reliance on technical effects, everything must be guaranteed to work reliably, otherwise it is not worth including in the show. With so many people and effects operating without visible contact with each other, one delay can ruin the most elaborate and expensive plans. For this reason it is much more of a director's theatre than smaller-scale work. A management team is needed to ensure the smooth running of the operation. It is not so open to improvisation or individual interpretation but is much more about teamwork. This also limits the amount of play that can happen with the public. There may be sections of the piece that allow for some interaction with the public but there is obviously not the same freedom of action that is enjoyed by the solo.

It is not absolutely essential to have a large group in order to achieve a big effect. The Inflatable Theatre Company performs to thousands of people in an area the size of a football pitch with a team of only six people. Once their 80-foot dragon has been dramatically inflated to its vast size, it can speed around the arena at 25 mph because it is mounted on a van. A simple human drama is enacted to give life to this massive effect. A plucky St George, complete with a real horse, does battle and manages to rescue a swallowed princess by cutting her out of the belly of the defeated dragon. The reduced human scale is thus used to good effect. Epic amplified music completes this simple but effective spectacle.

ORGANISING LARGE-SCALE EVENTS

This section is based on an interview with Robin Morley, who is a production and technical director for Zap Productions, based in Brighton. They are promoters themselves, bringing important foreign companies such as Archaos to Britain. They are also commissioned as programmers, consultants and organisers for outdoor theatre festivals, such as that of Streetbiz, Glasgow, in 1990.

> For outdoor theatre companies there are two parts to the work – first getting your own act together and second ensuring that the host organisation really understands what you are trying to do, that they have got their act together and that they will support you, because you are hugely dependent on them for the success of the project. Sometimes a host organisation has not got the breadth of imagination, or possibly enough resources, and that means the visiting company must take on their function as well. On the other hand, some of the more experimental companies have an ethos about spending almost all their time on their work and are not that interested in the concerns of production, administration and marketing. From the promoter's point of view these are difficult companies; they might miss press calls, which the promoter has spent a lot of time setting up, because they do not see the value of marketing.
>   The process of setting up a visit works in the following way. Initially the artist sends a proposal for a site or a situation to the host. Or the host invites the artist. Where the initiative comes from is most important. The host organisation has got to want you to come. Alternatively the arrangement might be much looser – the host organisation is simply providing the very important elements of marketing and the site in return for money through box-office receipts. A meeting might then be held with the local

promoter who provides a list of possible sites that fit the requirements of the visiting company – the size of the space, access for vehicles, electricity, water and sewerage. Discussions might also take place on the theme of the festival, whether or how the visiting company might fit in with this, whether there is any kind of community involvement and how this might operate. The promoter can facilitate the company, providing the site, rent free, and obtaining permissions but they must know what the visitors are going to do; if there is going to be a lot of noise they need to think about local reaction. Also the host needs to think about how many people are going to come to this event – if it is up to 13,000 it is going to be quite difficult to see at the back. One way to control numbers is by allowing entrance to the site by ticket only, even if they are free; this commits people to coming and prevents overcrowding. There could be a nominal charge but for many companies this would go against the idea of what they are trying to do.

The next stage is the concrete organisation of the project. A number of visits to the site would determine viewing points for the audience. Also determining what time of day the performance will take place will decide the quantity, type and positions of lighting. Site plans, pre-production and production schedules are drawn up. At this stage it is possible to tell how well the event is going to be from the level of communication between the two organisations. Of course, it is quite possible for the company to simply arrive and get on with it, as is the case with smaller-scale events, but in that case they have to be able to provide everything for themselves.

For anyone working in large-scale outdoor theatre it is important to be absolutely sure that the local authorities can understand and work with you, otherwise a situation may arise where they are trying to censor your show or change it. It is a full-time job for someone to sort all that out. In Britain the main concern of the health and safety officers is the audience rather than the performer. They are very worried if you do anything to or with the audience that puts spectators at risk. In France it is possible to do much more with the audience and this is a big problem for European groups coming to Britain. Royal de Luxe worked once in this country and it was a disaster for them; after that they said 'Never again'. In 1992 the EEC regulations come into force which, in some ways, makes it easier because in theory a licensed pyrotechnician can work anywhere in the EEC. However, each place has its own local conditions and there is now even a United Nations law about moving pyrotechnics around the country.

It is essential for visiting companies to build a level of trust with the local authorities so that they feel you know what you are doing, that you take your work seriously and that you are able to speak their language. When Archaos came to London, the fire officers were fine about it because they were given very good quality information about safety distances, and the sort of precautions taken. Once they feel that you are thinking in that way they are reassured, especially if they know you have done similar things elsewhere. Urban Sax, for example, frequently use buildings to abseil off; if they just go somewhere and say we are going to have someone abseiling down this glass panel they are going to be adamantly refused but if they can show they have done it on Cologne Cathedral and at Versailles, the owner of the building will know that they are not going to drill holes and that their concerns are going to be taken seriously.

Any large-scale public event generally has to have a public entertainments licence. It is not needed for smaller-scale street theatre. It is particularly for events such as rock concerts and there is even a 'Rock Code' of practice, which is to do with crowd control, emergency services, proper security and avoiding crushes. Particularly with large events, the requirements of the local safety regulations need to be considered at a very early stage, rather than conceiving the work first and then trying to fit in with the concerns of the police, fire and safety officers. This is a problem for French and Spanish companies because they are very insistent on the integrity of their work and much less compromising; their philosophy is 'We are here to change people's minds and to show them something they have never seen before'. In these countries there is a stronger tradition of anarchism and of using culture as a political tool. This attitude is fundamental to their work and can appear to be totally contrary to concerns for people's safety but in fact it is not. Most British groups are more negotiable.

There has to be a budget for sorting out all these production details. Deciding who does this work and who pays for it has to be negotiated at an early stage. The host might do all the production and simply give a fee for the performance; the host might be well placed to get better deals with local hire firms. Sometimes the host will give the money to the visiting company for them to sort out all their requirements. Alternatively the host might employ a third organisation to programme, produce and promote a range of visiting companies. In the case of Streetbiz, Zap Productions also generated more income by obtaining sponsorship in kind and in cash. Quite often these organisations have a better idea of which groups are appropriate to that particular festival.

The Welfare State Handbook, called *Engineers of the Imagination*, and edited by Tony Coult and Baz Kershaw, has more information on the staging of outdoor events including information on fire, the emergency services, insurance, stewarding crowds and the British legal complexities.

THÉÂTRE DU ROYAL DE LUXE: THE EPIC SPECTACLE

Royal de Luxe are the most well-established outdoor theatre group in France. The show they devised for the bicentennial of the French Revolution was a masterpiece of outdoor spectacle, making extensive use of effects that could not be used indoors. It was a self-contained show that toured over a few years, with usually at least a week in each place.

The performing area is large (about 24 metres square) with a separate musicians' area on one side. The team of about twenty spend the fifty minutes of the show in frantic activity, either onstage, or changing costume, or operating the many mechanical devices. By the end of the apocalyptic climax they all look as if they have indeed survived a battle as real as the one they were representing.

The show is called 'La Véritable Histoire de France' and consists of a collage of scenes from French history, not necessarily in chronological order and without any attempt to develop a theme. Its success is due to the interesting and imaginative way that the familiar scenes are represented. Joan of Arc is first shown dressed in fashion gear from the 1960s, in a picture-book landscape with two-dimensional pop-up sheep, where she is vacuum-cleaning the grass and keeping her world prim and neat. Two angels in underpants complete with automatic flapping wings appear astride a little rocket and they sing to her about her mission. In the next scene the set reveals an entire medieval castle under siege, being bombarded by various contraptions including a giant fork 3 metres long. When the castle is set on fire by a giant arrow, strips of red and yellow cloth, which are set into the castle, are animated by large fans blowing air upwards so that they look like flames. Joan's demise is shown with her harnessed to a horizontal spit rotating over more air-animated flames. This early sequence makes it clear to the audience that this history is going to be a quirky and slightly irreverent interpretation rather than a respectful homage to France's great people.

The stage consists of a series of flat sections, 7 metres by 5, laid on top of each other and hinged at the back like the leaves of a book. As each 'page' is winched to the vertical it reveals the backdrop for the next scene; at the end of the scene this is lowered backwards, so that the stage gradually gets lower, until the whole book has been turned over. In the final action of the piece, a huge spine cover is lifted into place and leaned against the outer edges of the 'pages' creating an epic sense of scale. This ingenious device allows for elaborate changes of set which would be easy to fly in inside a normal proscenium arch theatre but otherwise impossible to achieve outdoors. Each backdrop is different in style; the besieged castle looks as if it is from an illuminated manuscript, the seventeenth-century Age of Navigation is done with mechanical waves typical of the masque, the First World War is done with graphic realism and the 1930s is shown in the bold style of cartoons from the period.

It is the ingenuity of the effects that continually surprises and astounds the audience. The scientific discoveries of the eighteenth century are represented by the inflation and release of a beautifully constructed hot-air balloon that floats up and is released into the sky. Napoleon's siege of Moscow is shown by a vast flame-thrower which heats up a metal cut-out of the city and then buckets of water are thrown on to give a spectacular

Figure 14 Royal de Luxe: Napoleon burns Moscow

steam/smoke effect. At another moment a hundred mechanical birds are ejected from a special container to flutter briefly around the arena. The finale is an extraordinary battle sequence from the First World War in which all kinds of pyrotechnic devices are used including ones fitted into costumes to simulate the wearer's being shot. Hand-thrown fire crackers give the sound effect of machine-gun fire and, from behind the set, there are huge explosions, sending up clouds of dried peat that envelop the scene in a murky haze and cover the audience with a fine dust. By the end the audience has been bombarded by sight and sound and, with this covering of dust, they look, as well as feel, as if they have been through a real battle. This climax is more exhilarating than a simple firework display because it is accompanied by a real sense of danger, urgency and struggle, with the entire crew engaged at full energy.

Royal de Luxe combine the three essential ingredients of large-scale theatre – size, surprise and spectacle. The epic nature of the subject makes the large scale appropriate and justifies the amount of energy and expense. The episodic nature of the piece would present problems for normal theatre, but outdoors it is a real advantage because it gives them the opportunity to use so many different devices. As with so much spectacle, the visual effect is immediate and short-lived, so it is good to have a continual passage of different images. The nature of the subject makes character development inappropriate and although the 'King of France' makes an appearance at the beginning and end there is very little narrative through-line. The piece, therefore, cannot be judged in terms of conventional theatre. It is the designers, constructors and pyrotechnicians as much as the performers who get our applause at the end.

WELFARE STATE BURN THE HOUSES OF PARLIAMENT

The achievement of John Fox, Boris Howarth and the rest of the regular Welfare State workers has yet to be fully appreciated. Along with other groups like InterAction they have stimulated a whole new range of community theatre. Their premiss that theatre should be a product of the community rather than imposed from outside was shared by other influential contemporaries – Augusto Boal, the Living Theater and Odin Theatre – but it is Welfare State that has been most influential in Britain in generating a network, a method and a style which have become larger than the group itself.

Their base in Barrow, Cumbria has provided a site for their important summer schools which further their aim of passing on techniques to others and has created an infrastructure of community theatre that has greatly enriched the cultural life of the north of England. At Barrow they have explored their ideas of gently transforming an environment by discovering, enhancing and giving value to what is already there. In simple physical terms they have made a sculptural garden of a piece of 'ordinary' woodland. In commissioned projects they normally send some members two or three weeks in advance to discover local stories and traditions. They work with local people to give them ways of participating in the event so that when the rest of the group arrive the foundations are laid for a fruitful collaboration.

Although their rural base is a retreat they do not seek to cut themselves off from contemporary problems; Barrow has also given them a concrete and complex political issue to challenge

directly. The manufacture of nuclear submarines was the one
major local industry until the end of the cold war and without it
the unemployment rate would be as high as in other parts of the
blighted north of England. Welfare State did not shrink from
tackling this difficult and complex issue. They more or less
succeeded in treading the fine line between attacking the principle of making tools for mass destruction and alienating the
individuals who were not in an economic position to make fine
moral choices about where they worked. This is important as an
example of how it is possible to maintain a provocateur stance
while also retaining popular appeal. It takes a good deal of
sophistication to shock and challenge without alienating the
public.

The political stance of Welfare State originates in the radical
1960s and has not been seriously compromised since then,
although it may be toned down if there is a risk of alienation.
Their highly successful series of fire sculptures entitled 'The
Burning of the Houses of Parliament' was a typical example of
how they combine a popular tradition with a revolutionary
theme. They turned the Guy Fawkes story inside out; instead of
burning an effigy of the supposed villain they celebrated his
attempt by burning a symbol of what was actually more unpopu-
lar – the institution of politicians, the representation of the
Establishment. At the biggest of these spectacles, at Catford,
south London, in 1981, the image was accompanied by a sound-
track of 'Anarchy in the UK' by the Sex Pistols and 'Sympathy
for the Devil' by the Rolling Stones, a song rich in provocateur
imagery. Many of Welfare State's shows contain a revolutionary
theme of some sort, often linked to the death and resurrection
theme of the mummers' plays.

At that particular event they had spent at least two weeks
preparing the material and erecting the structure. The tower
representing Big Ben was as high as 13 metres and the width of
the whole set was at least 20 metres. It was perfectly situated on
top of a small hill in a park. Because the hill had a slightly
steeper rise at the top, it was possible to see nearly all the
structure over the heads of the people in front. This enabled the
15,000 people who watched it to get a reasonable view and
avoided a big crush at the front. A performance platform had
been constructed in the set so that the important human action
could be well seen before the bigger spectacle started. The

audience was kept clear of a large area around the structure by strong metal barriers and within this 'safety zone' tall, mobile puppet effigies were used as protagonists in a prelude to the main action. The giant figures of Margaret Thatcher and Guy Fawkes had actors appearing out of the top of their heads who harangued one another and the audience. Giant birds and a dragonfly were carried on vertical poles around the edge of the arena. An enormous stork, 5 metres high, carrying a bundle in its beak, traversed the area mounted on top of a car. A large sailing ship was manoeuvred into battle and set ablaze.

The focus now shifted to the main structure; the nature of the power of Parliament was suggested through shadow puppet images on screens in the set. Human figures were hung from gallows and at this point the music, which had been acoustic and mobile, changed to being amplified, pre-recorded and much louder. Devilish characters appeared from the jaws of a Hell's Mouth, one using a flame-thrower, another swinging a fire ball. A series of explosions started the fireworks concealed in the set and the structure began to burn. With the music and flames building up, an enormous skeleton, 12 metres high, was raised into position from behind. As the tower and the rest of the structure began to collapse magnificently (carefully controlled by metal cables), the best firework display I have ever seen began. It was beautiful and perfectly timed to fit in with the music. The emotional power of the songs and strong images turned a pretty display into a highly charged means of expression that left the audience exhilarated and literally 'fired up'. Most of them were local families who had not come to watch theatre but to watch a bonfire and some fireworks. They were amazed by it, on the level of simple spectacle, and certainly surprised, amused and impressed by the more theatrical elements of the event. Although they gained a lot of fans that night, this was the last time Welfare State staged this piece; they regarded it as too successful to be repeated.

Chapter 12

Site-specific work

All outdoor performers take some account of the location of their shows. However, some groups go much further and design the performance for a specific location. It might be that an already chosen theme needs an appropriate site; Lumiere & Son chose to do a show about the destruction of the rainforests and found an appropriate site in the grounds of London's Kew Gardens. Or more usually, it might be that the physical aspects of the place propose the theme itself. They become the vital participants in the performance, just as much as the actors. The Dutch group Dogtroep were commissioned to do a performance beside a canal in Rotterdam. They devised all kinds of ways of using the water.

> Objects which play a part in the rest of the performance are fished out of the murky depths with a wooden crane; two performers approach on a pair of rickety rafts hardly 3 square metres in size, wearing massive fire constructions on their heads – they turn through 90 degrees every time they step on their pedals. Between them is a third raft where a figure looking like Buster Keaton connects his black suit to a pump and is transformed into a living fountain; a 3-metre bright orange fish swims around by itself, propelled by an invisible diver; a rowing boat approaches and fires a harpoon, the fish is hauled out, suspended above the water by the cables that are hanging in the air, and it bursts open into a firework display.
>
> (from the Dogtroep annual report 1987–8)

IOU define this area of work in the following way.

The main difference with a show devised for a specific site rather than one devised to tour, is that the physical characteristics of the space condition the narrative, structurally and in content. The setting generates and shapes ideas. Shows are 'built in' to the place they are performed in. In a site-specific show, the relationship between theatre and 'reality' is changed. There may be a clear 'edge' – sometimes danger.

Welfare State go even further because their shows could be said to be audience-specific as well as site-specific. They devise their performances from the local culture, both historical and contemporary. At Northwich in Cheshire their advance party discovered that there were local salt mines still in operation. This led them to a story of a local worker whose hobby was to carve the abandoned caverns into exotic sculpture, thus creating his own fantastic subterranean world. This story, along with dead seas and the preservative quality of salt, gave them a rich imagery to work from. By bringing blocks of salt from the mine for other people to carve, they encouraged the continuity of a local tradition as well as celebrating one man's hidden genius.

For Welfare State it is not just the performance that is important, it is the process of bringing people together and passing on techniques to help them create and organise themselves. At Northwich the procession around town, earlier in the day, provided an opportunity for local participation as well as advertising the evening event. The group had set up in the park with tents, banners, windsocks and, after dark, a magical path of flickering lamps to lead in and out of the created environment. After the performance, food and drink were available and then a barn dance in which everyone was actively encouraged to participate. The group, therefore, tries to provide a whole night out; a fairground environment that is imaginative and different but familiar enough for the local people to make a safe place in which barriers can be broken down. So all the ingredients are designed to be appropriate to the particular site, the whole area and the specific audience.

Because site-specific shows cannot, by their very nature, tour, the prospective audience will be relatively limited in numbers. So, although the same amount of energy will have gone into creating the show as for a touring show, the 'life' of the show will be relatively short. This makes site-specific work fairly expensive. Bookers will also have to place a good deal of trust in the reputation of the group because there is no way the finished product can be seen before the contract is agreed. These two factors mean that there is certainly not as much site-specific work as there might otherwise be. Dogtroep, Welfare State and the Suffolk-based Company of Imagination get round this problem by bringing pre-devised material that is flexible enough to be rearranged to adapt to each specific location.

However, this kind of work does not have to be on a large scale. My Brazilian partner and I found ourselves doing shows at hotels along the coast of Kenya. We had various circus-type routines already worked out but we found that one particular hotel had a swimming pool in the shape of the African continent. During one day we devised a scenario with master and servant characters who were on safari around the coastline of the continent. Their relationship exaggerated the unequal status between the European tourists and the local people and this was very much appreciated by the hotel employees. A low wall separated the shallow lower end of the continent and we used this as the South African border with my Brazilian partner not being allowed in because of his darker skin colour. Coming up the west coast we decided to cut across the Sahara by swimming across it, crying out for water as if we were dying of thirst. We added various stunts like walking barefoot over a River Nile made of broken glass and falling from a tree that had been climbed to gather coconuts.

A journey scenario is obvious given a large map to play with, but often the site does not present such easy solutions. Over the last few years the Natural Theatre has provided theatrical entertainment for a long-distance bike ride from the northern tip of Scotland to the furthest extremity of Cornwall. Long stretches of small roads do not seem very inspiring but the Naturals have developed their own brand of 'hedgerow theatre'.

Panting up a narrow precipitous lane, closed in by woods, the unsuspecting bicyclist is likely to be suddenly confronted by two fern-draped soldiers with blackened faces charging out at him from each side of the road; an arrow-bedecked convict breaking stones with a sledge-hammer pleads with passers-by for a key to unlock his manacles and a man with a blunderbuss in his hand bobs up from a hedge making quacking noises every time a cyclist appears.

(Bettina Selby, 'Over the Sea to Skye')

In the middle of a boggy hillside Queen Victoria sits inappropriately with a guardsman in full regalia parading before her. A farmer had placed an old bath as a drinking trough for cattle. With a little adjustment and a happy occupant, complete with soap and loofah, the bath is returned to its former use. At a sign announcing the border into England the cyclists are greeted by a beer-swilling yob, complete with Union Jack shirt and a knotted handkerchief on his head. In a front garden, on a new housing estate in the Midlands, pose two real-life garden gnomes.

Ralph Oswick explains:

Each of the 100 scenarios in our repertoire is carefully planned. Some are stunts, some visual jokes, some complete scripted pieces and others memorable 'images' on a higher plane. Part of the 'art' is the attention to detail, part is choice of what to do where, part is the being able to repeat the action in a fresh and amusing way over and over again as the hundreds of cyclists meander by in dribs and drabs. Part of it is the surprise – the riders must never see us out of character or hiding our large and obvious van.

As can be seen the environment can be used in two ways – either going with it by using a wholly appropriate cliché like the garden gnomes, or going against it like the man in a bath in a field. This is also one of the key features of mobile shows.

IOU IN 'THE HOUSE'

IOU is based in Halifax and was founded in 1976 by a group of visual artists and musicians who wanted to work together exploring different ways of looking at paintings and sculpture and how these could be combined with music. Theatre was the most appropriate medium. They have devised shows for beaches, rivers, lakes, woods, churches, cathedrals, castles, disused houses, market-places, exhibition halls, mills, courtyards and rooftops.

The following extract is written by Steve Gumbley, one of the core members of the group.

'The House' was originally commissioned by Chapter Arts Centre in Cardiff, and a second version was produced for the Almeida Festival in London [1982]. In both shows a real house was used as a setting for ordinary and extraordinary human actions.

Outline description of the show

The audience was seated in the garden, positioned so they could see real events in the street beyond, as well as dramatic events staged in and around the house. This tension between real and make-believe was a strong element in the show.

Each performance began at dusk with the house inhabitants preparing for bed. The audience glimpsed a collage of action through the windows; a woman arguing with her son about homework, a man brushing his teeth, the milk bottles and the cat being put out for the night.

The appearance of an angel on the chimney-stack interrupts the prosaic chain of events. Music is heard. He descends to transform the garden, and is joined by two saints carrying bee-hives. Each weed they touch bursts into flower. Honey oozes from the hives, into the angels' hands . . .

From then on the story has a pure and vivid complexity. It is as though the house itself is dreaming, and the dream has taken over the house. At the same time there are real passers-by – kids, dog-walkers, kerb-crawlers and emergency vehicles which become an unselfconscious part of the action.

So, when a black Ford Corsair crashes into the garden shrubs, the audience has to wonder if it is a real accident or part of the dream. In fact the driver and his mate are two large 'bees' who have heard that their honey has been stolen. They stagger from the smashed car, angrily cursing their bruises. Wearing tea-strainer goggles and stuffed stripy shirts, they are a combination of bees and burglars. Armed with lump hammers and crowbars they force their way into the house, looting food and deck-chairs for a revengeful feast of outrageously sloppy sandwiches in the garden. Meanwhile . . . a policeman driving a 'police' lawn-mower (complete with radio and flashing blue light) arrives to investigate the crashed car. An arresting scene occurs.

The house is then taken over by a family of scribes who seem to be obsessed with rewriting history. There is a series of scenes in which they wash books, beat the pattern out of carpets, and shoot chairs. A coalman delivers in the dead of night.

The show ends with an airmail delivery; a postman in a light aircraft circles above the rooftop, and one of the scribes climbs a precarious 40-foot ladder to receive a brown paper parcel as the plane passes.

Devising the show

A site-specific show, such as 'The House', demands many weeks of very intensive work by a very good team. The diversity of the work involved requires a great amount of organisation, at all stages.

Areas of work

Administrative work begins twelve months or more in advance of the event and includes:

Initial contact with promoters
fundraising, sponsorship, grant applications
negotiating contracts to cover all details of fees and
    arrangements
planning site visits and meetings with promoters
contacting extra artists or workers
obtaining necessary permits and licences for show site
arranging accommodation
producing and distributing publicity
arranging any insurance that may be necessary
budgeting, book-keeping and payments
contacting press and TV, press releases, documentation.

Technical work includes:

making the site safe and secure
laying in electricity and water supplies
finding storage for equipment

hiring and rigging lights
hiring and erecting scaffolding (for rooftop scenes and
    lighting towers)
landscaping site to accommodate audience (In Cardiff a
    large brick wall was moved, in London the whole site
    was reshaped by a bulldozer.)
hiring and erecting raked seating
installation of safety lighting, steps and ramps
installation of toilets for site
rigging special effects
rigging sound amplification.

Ideas

As soon as a site is found, specific ideas can be developed
through discussions by the whole company. Individuals
develop own ideas and present them at regular meetings.
Swapping and modifying ideas continues throughout the
making of sets and objects. Performance ideas arise from
made objects, music and the overall scenario. Final shaping
and editing of the scenario occurs as late as possible. An
order of main scenes is decided; linking and bridging
scenes are then devised and rehearsed. Positions and cues
are agreed. When the set-building is complete, the lights
are focused and levels set. Fine-tuning of all elements can
occur in walkthroughs, dress rehearsal and throughout the
run of performances.

    Set and objects for 'The House' included:

building an exterior staircase to transform into a waterfall
conversion of a scrap car for 'bees' sequence
conversion of a lawn-mower into a police motor cycle
making about twenty costumes and many small props
redecorating house exterior and interior
making extra outbuildings and additions to the garden
building a 25-foot 'aircraft' and mounting it on a
    revolving hydraulic access crane.

Conclusion

On a project such as this, the workload is huge, and much of it has to happen in a few weeks. Resources will be stretched to their limits, whilst safety has to be prioritised. Having said that, site-specific shows produce the most exciting and memorable theatre.

Chapter 13

Mobile shows

There are three types of mobile show: the journeys in which the audience is guided through a series of different locations, the processions in which the audience remains static and watches images pass by; and finally the walkabout theatre in which the performers mingle with the audience.

The beauty of them is that the location is not fixed, which means that not just one but several can be used which provides continual stimulation from the changing conditions. The mobile show is also more able to reach an audience that would not normally go to watch theatre. As many people carry a fear or a prejudice towards outdoor theatre, they will not stop and watch a stationary show but there may be no way of avoiding a mobile show. They may come across it unexpectedly and it may even follow them.

JOURNEYS

Journeys have an ancient resonance; the thrill of the hunting expedition, the trials of the religious pilgrimage and the adventure of voyages of discovery. In our own day these have become replaced by the package tour, the ghost train and the magical mystery tour. All these elements feed into the themes of theatrical journeys. The hunt has become a quest for clues to solve a mystery, Els Commediants' journey is through a Hell reminiscent of Dante's spiritual journey, Guirigai base their performance on a conquistador expedition of the seventeenth century. In all these scenarios there is a thrill of discovery and wonder at the unknown.

There are many different types of theatrical journey but the one thing they all have in common is that the audience must move in order to see the show. Nearly always there are a number of set-piece, static scenes interspersed with the actual journey. This movement of the audience is usually accompanied or assisted by the performers. In some cases the audience not only has to make this effort, it also has to place considerable trust in the performers because it may be transported away from familiar surroundings with no easy possibility of opting out.

Red Earth devise the journey from the surroundings in the manner of site-specific work and most groups will use the available surroundings to some extent, although this is not absolutely necessary. The Délices Dada journey, described later (pp. 153–5), could be set up in any suitable outdoor situation. This makes it unnecessary to adapt the show for each different location, but it does miss out on the exciting possibilities presented by each place. Most groups will use the method, already mentioned, of having an adaptable scenario so that they can make some use of surroundings without having to devise a whole new piece for each different venue.

Emergency Exit has done a number of journeys, one on a boat down the Thames. This included action in the boat, on the passing shore, and in and out of the water – a mermaid appeared alongside the boat and later climbed aboard. They have also done a couple of mini-journeys at Christmas time, along the lines of the traditional Santa's Grotto. One was installed inside a disused supermarket and the other on a coach. They gutted the coach and created a complete environment inside it. Three or four children were taken through at a time and told a story as they moved between different tableaux.

Theatrical journeys fall into three different categories, each with its own advantages and disadvantages in relation to sightlines and timing. The first is the one in which the whole audience follows the actors, who travel through a series of different scenes, much like a static play only in different locations. The Spanish group Guirigai, described below (pp. 152–3), fall into this category. This method has the advantage that the timing is dependent on the actors. However, Guirigai's journey through the streets of Aurillac was followed by a huge number of spectators that crowded the action making it very difficult to see the actors, except where they used a raised stage or a natural amphitheatre like the park pond. Over-zealous photographers competed for close-up shots and actually placed themselves amongst the actors. Barriers would have impeded the progress of the spectators along the narrow streets and therefore prevented them from following the sequence of scenes. Stewards would have had a difficult time keeping the audience back, because the actors were often quite separate from one another. Obviously, there is no way of knowing exactly how big will be the following crowd but with free, unlimited access large numbers can be expected if the journey is done in the centre of town. It is also necessary to try to foresee how much they are willing to give the actors space.

The second tactic is where the audience moves to watch scenes in different places without necessarily being led. Els Commediants use this tactic, often with fireworks to indicate the next point of the journey or even to goad people forward. The performance does not have such a concentrated centre of focus so the audience does not crowd in so tightly. Els Commediants use a combination of large set-pieces, best seen from a distance, and some manic mingling amongst the crowd that helps to move the people and to splinter the focus. However, moving a crowd of hundreds or thousands over a large area creates problems of timing and co-ordination. Audience members move at different paces so it is difficult to create surprising effects with impact if the audience is very spread out. This is why Els Commediants use the fast-moving minglers (on roller-skates when I saw them) because they can appear suddenly from out of the surrounding crowd.

The other way to create surprise is by funnelling the audience through a channel, with hidden actors or inanimate images only revealed close-up, much in the same way as a ghost train. Lumiere & Son used this at Kew Gardens by having actors in elaborate animal and insect costumes hidden in trees and bushes. This works well, except that moving the audience through takes some time, so that there has to be an ongoing event at the end of the channel that keeps the interest without developing the action too much, otherwise those at the back will have missed necessary information. It would be possible to end the performance at the end of the channel but usually most groups like to end with a set-piece finale, watched by everyone. This is because the channel system, much like the Natural Theatre's bike ride (pp. 138–9), only permits very brief sequences that can be repeated many times.

The third possibility is the magical mystery tour in which audience groups of limited numbers are guided by the actors through a series of staged events. This tactic enables there to be a more intimate contact and interplay between the performers and audience, so they can be included in the action – there is a pretext for their journey. By limiting the numbers (from 30 up to 200 is possible), it is possible to ensure good sight-lines, to conceal surprises along the route and to perform longer sequences at each stop. Even this method has its problems, however, because the audience groups need to have the guidance between set-pieces animated in some way in order to keep the performance continuous. Red Earth created their journey in a beautiful wood. Although this had the advantage of some wonderful natural settings, the narrow paths meant that there was a long single line of spectators, with the more agile and enthusiastic children racing ahead. Again, there was a waiting time at each halt while the less agile caught up. Even where the paths are wider and the whole group can move in a block it requires skill to keep the performance continuous. The essential ingredient is to have at least one performer who can keep in character and improvise endlessly while also being able to cope with problems and control events. This role can be passed on from one 'guide' to another but maintaining it is particularly important where the audience is in unfamiliar surroundings, otherwise the spectators will start to worry about the means of exit rather than allowing themselves to enjoy the illusion being created. Welfare State manage to animate these sections of movement with a combination of live music, static images *en route*, 'guides' and sometimes the invitation to participate by carrying lanterns or processional images.

In most theatrical journeys the role of the audience remains that of passive spectator. This is a shame because they are perhaps the ideal means for audience participation since the spectators have already agreed to participate by walking, and have already shown trust in the performers by putting their movements under the control of the group. In this way journeys can be seen as a form of mass-animation. The French group Opposito creates an animated journey by setting up a game of bull-fighting between a massive bull puppet and toreadors on stilts. The bull keeps breaking out of the performing area and the audience has to scatter as it charges towards them. There is a chase through narrow streets, accompanied by fireworks; all this creates an atmosphere of light-hearted confusion in which the audience is either being chased or is running to see the centre of excitement. Other forms of involvement are less hectic; with Délices Dada they are all on a secret mission to hand over the package; Red Earth's journey is an investigation into a mystery. These are very effective ways of involving the whole audience; even though they know it is only a pretence it still adds to the adventure of discovery.

Apart from animators the other artistic group this format appeals to is that of the performing artists. The possibility of constructing static images, in order to create different environments, appeals to sculptors, lighting designers and other visual artists. For groups like Red Earth the 'sculpture trail' aspect of the event takes at least as much time to devise as the performance. The possibility of creating a total sensory experience, including those of smell, taste and touch, is an exciting prospect. Unlike in a normal spectating situation, the audience is physically enclosed within the play. Imaginative museums, such as the Jorvik Viking Centre at York, use total environments. Outside a real environment can be used rather than an artificial one and this is an area of work that I believe could see much development in the future.

RED EARTH JOURNEY TO THE WHORLD STONE

Red Earth spent three weeks in a beautiful hilltop wood near their home town of Brighton, creating their site-specific journey, called 'The Whorld Stone'. Most of the preparation period was devoted to making sculptures and other constructions at carefully selected areas throughout the wood. The materials used were almost entirely natural; for example, masks were made out of bark, moss, leaves, feathers and wood.

The audience pays for tickets and is limited to forty. The spectators assemble just outside the wood and are led up to the starting point, which is a small marquee. At the appointed time we are crowded into the perfumed and dimly lit tent which contains many varied and unusual objects, reminiscent of anthropological specimens or natural curiosities in an old fairground booth. The tent door is firmly closed and we are

Figure 15 Red Earth involving the audience in their mystery

welcomed by a showman/master of ceremonies who, with a well-scripted speech, introduces us to the history of particular items. This is the collection of a Professor Whelpdale who mysteriously disappeared a long time ago with his daughter. There is a wardrobe called the Weirdrobe and also a kind of sphere called the Whelpdale Meteorite. It is said the professor disappeared when attempting to split the Meteorite and in true showman style the MC announces his intention to try to do the same before our very eyes. At the crucial moment the lights go out and, with smoke and strobe lighting, the doors of the Weirdrobe fly open and strange masked creatures come through them. When normal lighting is restored, the showman has disappeared with half the meteorite. With the help of his assistant we examine the Weirdrobe and discover a way through into a tunnel. The assistant asks us if we are prepared to go and look for the answer to the various mysteries that have been quickly set up. Having agreed, we enter a tunnel made of twigs and split branches. It is so low that it is necessary almost to crawl. Along the way are broken mirrors.

By this stage we are fully committed to the journey. We have voluntarily entered the transition space of the semi-magical marquee and one door has closed behind us. The second passage through the Weirdrobe makes it clear we are leaving the real world and should be prepared for anything. The well-written script and precise timing of the opening sequence give us enough confidence in the group to put ourselves in their hands. The first tunnel section makes it clear that the journey may be uncomfortable.

At the end of the tunnel we are welcomed into the other world by a reassuring lady in Victorian clothes, the professor's daughter, who is surprised to see us and asks us why we have come and what we know of the story so far. One of the audience has been entrusted to carry the half of the Meteorite and, seeing that, she offers to guide us on the search for her father and the showman. The pretext for the story is that in this other world there are some evil metallic creatures who have repressed other woodland creatures; the downtrodden can only recover their power by joining together the two halves of the Meteorite or Whorld Stone and restoring it to its proper place in the centre of the Whorl. All this only becomes clear as we pick up new information along the route.

We have to hide from two evil police guards on a motor bike. We have a sense that this other world is not only strange but hostile too. Further down the trail we come across a puppet booth made of branches in which part of the story is enacted by means of shadow and rod puppets. At another stop the daughter finds traces of her father and we all have to search for a number of marked stones in order to gain more information. In a hollow amongst big fallen trees, we have to hide behind a wall and witness two buffoon cooks, in their outdoor kitchen, arguing as they prepare to cook the showman, whom we can see in a cage strung up in a tree. At the next stop, we see the lords of the metal creatures seated round a table waiting to be served the cooked showman but he escapes and takes over the guiding of the group. We find a yew tree with a spiral of moss around it and lanterns in the branches. He gives us new information and leads us on to where we hear strange music and begin to see the shy, woodland creatures appear, playing whistles and drums, bringing their half of the Stone. Finally, we arrive at a spiral sculpture and the two halves of the Stone are joined together and placed on top of the spiral. A huge female puppet rushes out of the wood to show that the Whorld has been saved and our mission completed. We return via another short tunnel to the real world.

In the bright afternoon sun, with the light shafting through the trees, this was impressive enough but at night it became a very special experience. Natural light was used almost entirely; some scenes had a large fire to illuminate them while others were small and intimate enough to use only a single hurricane lamp. Hand-held fire torches bathed the strange images with a magical glow. The short range of the light from fire torches meant that all around there was darkness so that lights and sound were the only means the audience had to guide it through the wood. After a short time it became impossible to opt out because all sense of direction was lost and there were no available personnel to show the way out. The route was narrow and difficult in places, which meant that there were long periods of waiting at some of the stops, but the less agile had to make sure they kept up, otherwise they would have been left behind. The lack of bearings heightened the awareness of sound, touch, smell and sight, increasing the effectiveness of each new sensation. Forced to be alert in this way, and combined with the active involvement in the suspense of the story, the audience forgot the outside world and enjoyed a very vivid experience. Even though the pretext was fantastic and clearly aimed at younger people, older ones returned to the normal world with a slight sense of relief but also one of having been to another world. In this sense it is not unlike real travelling and real spiritual journeys – normal ways of experiencing and dealing with the world do not apply and new ones have to be learned.

GUIRIGAI JOURNEY TO ELDORADO

Teatro Guirigai performed their 'Voyage to Eldorado' at the 1990 Aurillac Festival. All the actors wore full-face, naturalistic masks and they were costumed in the style of the seventeenth century. There were seven characters: soldiers, a priest, aristocrats and court ladies. The route was right through the centre of town with a number of pre-set fixed constructions.

The starting point was at a bridge overlooking a weir. Here the audience had a good view of the river and at the appointed time a firework upstream announced the start and whereabouts of the initiating actions. Through a haze of coloured smoke two boats emerged carrying the characters already described. They slowly and elegantly disembarked and made their way to a vantage point, where they set up a cross and the priest gave a blessing. A long strip of elasticated material had been strung high up between two lines of trees. The group now separated into a single file and walked down this long strip, their weight pulling it down to the ground, with the elasticity raising it up in the spaces between them. This gave an effective representation of a mountain journey. At the end of it, there was a raised stage on which they discovered and silently devoured a prepared feast. Passing down a narrow street an assistant showered them with a bucket of granules. They sliced their way through a large sheet barrier and arrived at a coffin. When this was opened several real birds flew out. Eventually they arrived at the small park in the centre of town where the fountain in the middle of the pond had been dressed as a huge straw effigy; as they approached it across a gangplank a series of explosions set it on fire. Finally they arrived at the town hall and discovered a pyramid at the top of the steps. When this was turned around a bored man was revealed inside, slumped in front of his television. The message presumably being that this is the end result of the never-ending search for affluence.

The bucket of granules, the birds in the coffin, the pyrotechnics in the straw effigy and even the television man enlivened the journey with the all-important element of surprise. This was important because the characters, once seen, did not surprise or change. Also, the pre-set constructions could be seen before they arrived. The show worked best where there was distance between actors and audience – the big images at the river, the flaming effigy and the final sequence. However, because the performers could not relate to the audience within the context of the piece, the close proximity was unhelpful. In these sorts of situations the immediate presence of the audience must not only be acknowledged, but used as a positive advantage.

DÉLICES DADA: THE SURREAL JOURNEY

Délices Dada are a French troupe who, as their name suggests, use the surreal absurdity that was the legacy of the Dada movement.

The journey as it was performed at the Aurillac Festival in 1990 starts in a small pre-fabricated hut in the corner of a park. The hut is decorated like a kind of hunting lodge and at the appointed time a man in riding gear blows a hunting horn and then admits a limited number of people (about thirty) into the hut. Once inside, the door is locked and he welcomes us to the secret meeting of the followers of Doctor Claude Coussinet. We are obviously all dedicated followers of the famous doctor by the fact of having come to the meeting. We recite the code word of the secret society and agree to abide by its regulations. The President of the Association (the man in the hunting gear) reads out the Articles of the Association. He then inspects us in order to choose the person who is to be entrusted with carrying the secret sealed package. The feeling inside the tightly packed hut, with this crazy unpredictable man, is intimate to the point of being claustrophobic. We are in his hands now and there is no escape. He sends us on our mission to deliver the envelope and explains that we will be passed on to another Member of the Association further along the way. He sends us out through a false panel at the back of the hut, through a hole in the park fence and out into the street. Wondering where to go next we see an arm waving a little flag sticking out of a doorway further down the street. The figure emerges, dashes across the street, frantically indicating us to follow, and then disappears round a corner; bemused, we follow.

Meanwhile the next batch of audience waiting outside the hut is being allowed to enter, wondering how the previous group had disappeared from a hut with no obvious exit. Each group is met and guided further along the journey by a series of very odd characters, who tell stories of the great Claude Coussinet and the important effect he had had on their lives and on world events. One of these characters is found in the back of a medical van undergoing some form of sonic therapy (under a converted hair-drier). When he has emerged and delivered his semi-delirious rant he is locked back in the van by two medical orderlies. One of them leads us round a couple of corners, explaining, very matter-of-factly, the diagnosis and treatment of his crazy patient and making fun of his delusions. He at least seems normal. That is, until he starts to explain about how his patient had passed on one good tip that had been learnt from some bloke called Coussinet. He says he didn't believe it at first but thought he'd give it a try. It involves taking a sprig of parsley and sticking it in his ear. He demonstrates and says he can hear the tiny subterranean sounds of the garden just like you hear the sea in a shell. He starts to describe the sound of worms digging through the soil, a slug sliding over the surface, the seed beginning to sprout, and as he continues to talk he starts to go off into a hallucinogenic orgasm. When it's over he takes the parsley out of his ear and asks us what happened, saying it had been a wonderful experience and would we like to try it. Finally he looks round furtively and offers to sell us his stash, 'It's good quality stuff!' The last character we meet opens the package and inside are invitation cards to a soirée that evening at which the great Dr Coussinet may actually be present. The mystery continues.

All the performances are very well acted and scripted – played with very serious conviction. This makes the crazy logic very funny. The piece works so well because we are included in the game. At every stop we must recite the code word and pass on information we have learnt earlier in the journey. The actors use a very direct one-to-one contact that demands our total attention. From the moment of being locked in the hut we have to go along with the journey, united in conspiracy against normal society; indeed we are curiously observed by passers-by. Like any secret society, we relish their ignorance of our shared logic. It might be quite scary if we were not in a group and this slight intimidation pulls the group together. We are excited by the mystery which leads us on – what will be behind the next corner, what surprises will the next character come out with? Each of them possesses a different kind of craziness but they are united by the strength of their conviction.

Chapter 14

Processions

The procession is one of the oldest forms of outdoor theatricality. As an integral part of all ritual it could be said to be as old as religion itself. Traditionally it has two main aspects – the symbolic and the educational. In ritual, the sacred objects are displayed in close physical proximity to the worshippers. These may be functional objects such as chalices or objects of worship such as a cross. The educational aspect offers a reminder (but not a telling) of an important religious story – tableaux from the lives of gods or saints. At a later stage these static, silent tableaux began to be animated with movement and speech, leading to the simple dramas of the mystery and miracle cycles of medieval Europe. The aims of the religious authorities were much the same as those of today's outdoor theatre communicators; that is, to take out to the ordinary people that which is usually hidden away inside and shown only to an elite. So popular appeal through size and spectacle is an important element in procession.

The secular version of the religious procession was the pageant, a display of community or national identity. Like religious processions these would often include representation or personification of abstract values, such as Victory, the Virtues and Hope. This element can be seen in processions such as that of AFIC described below (pp. 159–60). Nowadays, pageant-type processions usually consist of motorised floats but they still retain their aim of community sharing, both in terms of construction and animation and also in their use in collecting money for charities. Processions are not only used for the promotion of moral or religious beliefs; the political march and the military parade are used as a display of power as well as to advertise an ideology. This advertising function is used by many outdoor theatre companies to promote the main show, much in the way old circuses used to parade through town.

There are some interesting companies who make or have made a journey by foot between places where they present shows. They almost always work in rural areas and, by travelling so slowly, simply and ostensibly, they find they can make contact with people who would not normally go and see theatre. Sometimes the shows are presented in exchange for hospitality or, in some cases, for a performance of local songs and dances. Odin Theatre were keen to develop this 'barter' of culture. The Polish group Gardzienice actually developed their style through contact with the traditional culture of remote rural communities. These groups acknowledge their position as outsiders and will often try to find ways of fitting in with local traditions, such as a musical style, or local preoccupations; when Horse and Bamboo, which is based in Lancashire, travelled round the Scottish islands they adopted the theme of boats and sailors and used traditional Scottish music styles.

The contact with local people will also be practical – Horse and Bamboo would need to find grazing for their horses (and occasionally a blacksmith) as well as suitable places to set up camp each night. All the activities on the journey become theatrical because the group is so constantly visible; it is constantly presenting its way of life, organisation, values and culture to the population in which it travels. In this sense it is like a long procession. In the case of Gardzienice, there is a missionary quality – however much they feel they receive from the environment, they also wish to contribute to the cultural life of those communities by introducing their own, more sophisticated artistic ideas. At the other extreme, the Strolling Players, based in Exeter, approach their audience much more from the level of lowly entertainers. For all these groups there is a desire to make contact on an ordinary, everyday level, to meet and get to know local people as well as bringing to them their gift – the performance.

Processions are different from journeys in that the audience does not move. There is a sequence of images that can be appreciated from one vantage point. Narrative is almost impossible because the audience cannot follow characters through different scenes. (The narrative in the mystery cycles was enabled because there were short stationary enactments which were moved around the town.) What is most important in a procession is the strength of the images. If there is a dramatic conflict it is between the whole procession and the surrounding environment. Groups like Malabar and Generik Vapeur use it in this way as a sort of 'invasion' of the streets. Before describing their work it is useful, for once, to look at a traditional procession in order to compare it with theatrical equivalents.

THE HEILIGDOMSVAART AT MAASTRICHT

The Heiligdomsvaart procession has taken place every eight years for centuries. It is a huge display of civic pride as well as being a religious event. Thousands of people are involved, either by taking a part in the actual procession or in the careful design and making of the colourful costumes and constructions. Not only is there size and spectacle but there is also live music in the odd combination of brass bands and choral hymn singing. Finally the synchronised marching gives the powerful effect of mass choreography.

It originated in the Middle Ages as a display of sacred relics around the town. These would normally have been kept locked away, so it was (and still is) a way of allowing people to come into close contact with the saints. The relics are accompanied by an image of a saint, either a sculpted 'portrait', or a living tableau of a scene from the saint's life. One is shown as a sailor on a ship with arms raised as if receiving a vision. The statue of another is entombed in a partially broken casket with a medieval soldier pointing his sword inside the casket. (Because the saint must face forward the unfortunate soldier had to walk backwards along the entire route.) In the same way the crucifix is an illustration that signifies the rest of the story; it becomes a symbol on which to focus faith. To an outsider these symbols may have no meaning; for example, one man reverentially carried a coconut. A cross, by itself, conveys no meaning if its significance is not understood.

The image of each saint is carried by the tradespeople associated with it – bakers, painters, carpenters, farmers and gardeners, all indicated by their tools or even their produce. This system helped the ordinary people identify with their own personal saint and encouraged the sense of participation in the event; pride and even competition between the groups is very much a feature of these community processions. More modern processions such as that of the Bridgwater Carnival are organised by neighbourhoods, often centred on pubs, rather than by professions. However, the sense of participating and sharing is more profound in a religious procession. Prayers are being spoken and hymns are being sung, so it is like a mobile religious service: bearing witness to the images together and sharing their significance unites the spectators.

So this procession has four functions; it can be seen as a show of strength to outsiders; it is a confirmation of identity through sharing an event, not only with contemporaries but also with the ancestors (in the sense of time-honoured tradition); it has an educational function, with its reminders of spiritual people; and finally it works on the level of simple theatrical spectacle. In India a Hindu temple also works on many levels simultaneously. For the children there is the temple elephant to make friends with, there are flashing lights and music to enjoy within the compound; for the intellectuals there are talks, for others there is meditation, for the physical there is ritual washing and yoga, for those who prefer an emotional relationship with the gods there are the many different statues to identify with; and finally there is the fundamental mystic level embodied in the anointed lingam-yoni symbol. Taken together in one evening all these elements provide something for everyone much in the same way as Heiligdomsvaart in Maastricht.

AFIC PERFORM 'CORPUS'

The large group of mainly young people in AFIC comes from Catalonia. The title of the performance refers, in Spain, to not only the day of Corpus Christi but also the procession itself. In effect, they use the format of the religious procession to convey a completely different meaning.

From seven o'clock in the morning pale, silent figures in shabby grey suits could be seen wandering around town carrying black plastic dustbin bags. At first glance they looked like tramps but gradually more appeared, either walking like zombies or just standing, staring into space, or even curled up asleep on the pavement in quiet corners. One tries to read a book, another stands on a box as if about to make a speech but no words come out. They regard us with reproachful eyes or perhaps they are desperately pleading behind their imposed silence. A 'factory' is set up – a circle of people with stacks of newspaper screwing each sheet into little balls and then throwing them on to what becomes a huge pile in the middle. After a certain time they fill a plastic bag and wander off only to be replaced by others. This is mindless work rewarded by useless earnings. They are uncomfortably similar to the lost souls in a real city.

Suddenly the procession appears and these strange characters slowly leave their positions and start to follow on behind. The procession is led by a child bride with a middle-aged groom. Young children, in similar grey suits, carry bouquets of dry flowers. Behind these there are about ten figures carrying emblems of their trade – a girl carries a rack of test-tubes, a gardener pushes a wheelbarrow, there is a businessman and a nurse. The impression is that not only do they represent trades but they are also allegorical figures – the girl with the test-tubes is Science, and so on. All these figures convey sterility and lifelessness; the wheelbarrow contains produce wrapped in cellophane, the pram contains a plastic baby. Then follows the centrepiece of the whole procession; a huge eyeball, 5 or 6 metres high, covered with a gauze shroud and carried at shoulder height on a bier. This 'god' is protected by ceremonial guards, much in the same way as in a real religious procession, except that these are sinister Space Age characters with reflecting sunglasses, silver tunics and riot truncheons. There is a near naked, silver-skinned attendant to the 'god' who taps out a doleful rhythm with two metal bars. At the back are the group of followers with plastic bags who grimly trudge in silence with their eyes on the ground.

Although some of the allegorical meaning is rather obscure, the feeling given is absolutely clear and very powerful. In the way of other communicators they take contemporary life and represent it from a different viewpoint. In this case they present a bleak view of the future, one of brain-washed oppression and technological sterility.

FRENCH ROCK THEATRE

Malabar, Generik Vapeur and Archaos all have a style which, like Fuera dels Baus, is tough, dangerous and accompanied by powerful rock music. It is futuristic and anarchic. This style is becoming very popular all over Europe. It is a blend of Spanish pyrotechnic effects, *bande dessinée* fantasy and French working-class rawness. Like punk in its early years, it is aggressive and has the same dynamic vitality. Although the style is more suited to younger people, older ones can become exhilarated by the danger and anarchy if they are not too alienated by the loud noise, wild appearances and bizarre behaviour. Although similar in style these three groups are different in the type of show they produce. Archaos work in a tent and so do not come within the scope of this book; Generik Vapeur are provocateur/ communicators concerned with content whereas Malabar are more involved in spectacle involving circus skills.

Malabar meet Mad Max

Malabar is a large group based in Montpellier, France. In 1989–90 they were touring several different types of performance; the procession, a battle spectacle called 'Face to Face', an outdoor rock opera and an 'aquatic theatre musical' called 'The Monkey'. The procession is a minor part of their work but as it is often used to advertise their other shows it is usually the first glimpse the public will get of them.

Even before they come into view their music can be heard; the centrepiece of this procession is an armoured truck with a huge train-type fender welded on to the front and a large circular structure on the bonnet which is used later. On the top of the van is a four-piece band – drums, electric guitar and keyboard. The rhythm is powerful and driving. As well as the music, intermittent explosions of fire-crackers can be heard. These are set off by about seven other characters who run, slither, acrobat, stilt-walk, or juggle fire around the van. All the characters are dressed in a kind of reptilian, Space Age armour, streaked from head to toe with red. A character on stilts rides an extended motor bike. He roars up, brakes suddenly and goes into a wheelie. Flares, coloured smoke and lines of petrol are ignited along the road. On passing a petrol station two characters rush over and caress the pumps reverentially. The post-holocaust world of Mad Max is not far away. They are wild-eyed, demonic and unpredictable – a modern version of medieval devils.

This procession led directly to a show in a castle. Their

purpose was to draw a crowd with them rather than present all their images *en route*. As soon as the van had been installed the space was cleared by dropping a few fireworks. With so much danger around, the crowd is alert and ready to move aside quickly; many of the entrances are through the crowd. More spectacular violence followed; a figure enters with his head protected by a kind of shell, his bodysuit is covered with lines of firecrackers; somebody ignites him and immediately this human firework almost disappears in smoke and sparks, as he turns in all directions. Two stilted warriors, with batons and metal shields, bash and kick each other until one is down and the other is fought by a woman wielding a long fire torch. From the back of the crowd another figure on stilts enters with two huge horns on a helmet/canopy. These horns are ignited and the whole area is showered with sparks, a woman is strapped to the metal circle and starts to rotate violently as the finale of smoke, sound and sparks rises to its climax.

The spectacle is exhilarating because of the obvious danger of the effects but also because of the sense of threat exuded by the performers. They all seem physically skilled and with their protective armour are like some tribe of warriors from a post-holocaust wasteland. Like all stunt work the effects look a lot more dangerous than they actually are but obviously, in this kind of show, it takes a high level of expertise in pyrotechnics, construction, circus skills and crowd control to have an acceptable level of risk of very serious injury.

Generik Vapeur roll out the barrel

The procession of Generik Vapeur in 1989 was very similar to that of Malabar. A centrepiece vehicle was covered with pipes and tubes and surmounted by a stage carrying a small rock band. Round about, a group of performers set off fireworks and did crazy things. The performers were streaked with colour – this time a deep blue. There was even a repetition of the Mad Max preoccupation with oil; their main show in 1989 was called 'Cafe Gazoil' and featured a petrol pump which was treated like a god. That year, they used oil barrels extensively both in the show and on the procession. The similarity between the groups was unfortunate although it is not clear how it came about. However, Generik Vapeur's show 'Délit de Sale Gueule', a year later, was markedly different; it was a bleak representation of modern city life with its faceless commuters, terrorism and latent militarism.

For both the procession and 'Café Gazoil' the oil barrels were a great asset. In the show, about a hundred were used to build a massive pyramid. In the streets they became percussion instruments, weapons and even vehicles – the performers would set up a line and then dive along them. The insistent drumming, the boom and rumble of the barrels as they were hurled or kicked forward was very powerful in the narrow streets of Aurillac because the sound was confined.

The performers wear suits and ties but their hair and faces are caked with what looks like blue mud. An older fat man pushes a smaller barrel on wheels with a dog's head and tail welded on. He ignites flares and throws them inside so that the slits on its belly glow brightly; with a chain lead he drives it forward. At one point these buffoons stop for a weird picnic using their barrels as tables. The fat man cracks an egg on the rump of his hot metal dog and then sucks it up with a straw as it begins to cook. Others produce lettuce and other raw eggs, which they devour revoltingly, while parodying polite behaviour. They are like aliens mimicking human behaviour without understanding it.

Like Malabar's procession there is a sense of invasion by an alien tribe. They do not relate directly to the public except to brush them aside like a conquering army. With both processions the drama is created by the risks they take. There is no apology, timidity, or politeness. Like all provocateurs they are not worried about offending or alienating people, they make a bold statement and if the residents of those narrow streets do not like the invasion then the disruption is only temporary. In this way they turn the briefness of the appearance with the static public into a positive advantage.

The processions of Malabar and Generik Vapeur were particularly effective because they dominated the environment with the volume of their sound and the uncompromising force of their activities.

PRACTICALITIES OF PROCESSIONS

Although not all groups will want to dominate the streets in quite this way it is important to be able to be seen as a coherent

Figure 16 Figure from Generik Vapeur's procession

identity. As has already been stated, a large number of people moving together is very impressive, so, however dispersed the activities, costumes should be united in style and colour. Even if numbers are not large, size and height can increase the effect. Stilts and banners are useful, a tall image can be seen from a distance and gives a central focus for the group. The route needs to be thoroughly examined, well beforehand, for any problems or possibilities but also there need to be 'front runners' immediately ahead to check for any changes or unexpected opportunities such as Malabar's petrol station. Generik Vapeur ran into difficulties because cars had been parked at the last minute, preventing the passage of their truck. Stewards can assist in this way and may be able to deal with problems better because they are not in costume or do not have the restriction of staying in character.

Audience interaction is difficult because the exchanges can only be brief and there are usually too many spectators to make contact with them all. What can be useful is contacting selected groups along the route: wearing dog masks on a particular procession we found we could get an interesting reaction from real dogs. Young children could be targeted in a similar way. The other problem with audience contact is that the performers become too dispersed, so that any kind of coherent image is lost. It is important therefore to keep a central focus otherwise the majority of the spectators will have nothing to look at while everyone is busy interacting on an intimate level. Also, if there is dispersal, there need to be clear signals for regrouping. Percussion helps to unite a group, music can give even more of a flavour. Obviously any amplification requires a vehicle for electricity but this can be unwieldy; brass instruments are more adaptable but there is the problem of lip-stamina on long processions. Experienced street bands learn how to give themselves rests while keeping the sound going. At its simplest the percussion plays on its own, then the brass on its own and then both together. This can give a powerful swelling effect and give variation without requiring too many tunes.

It is essential that the performers maintain a level of acting and do not just walk. They may not be engaged in frantic or extrovert activity – they may only be required to carry a banner, but they must hold an interior sense of purpose in whatever they are doing. Good processions have similarities to the structure of a static performance. The front runners introduce the theme which is developed in the middle part. The most powerful image is towards the end. The back is as important as the front; too often they only look good from the front and sides. If the large, central image comes just in front of the end of the procession, it is possible to hide a surprise or joke to round off the whole presentation. The effect of retreating can be as powerful as that of advancing.

Chapter 15

Walkabout

The third form of mobile show is the most common. It is called walkabout, mingling, or infiltration, according to the nature of the motive. It is perhaps the most important because it has no historical antecedents, except perhaps in the unstructured meanderings of costumed characters, which is a feature of some types of carnival.

Because there is no set-up, walkabout theatre can occur in places where theatre is not normally encouraged, such as shops and other places of work. The disruptive effect produced is very attractive to those with provocateur tendencies. The interaction with the spectators will be quite different from a static show. It will be a much briefer exchange and more on a one-to-one basis. There can be more room for play than in a stationary show in which the boundary between performer and audience is clearly delineated. The required mobility means it is necessary to operate without encumbering props and equipment so there will be more of an emphasis on character, costume and improvisation since these are the only available tools.

BASIC METHOD AND FINANCES

Unlike all other types of theatre the performer will aim to keep the number of spectators small, preferring a brief, intimate interaction and moving on if the crowd becomes too big or a particular action too long. In some rare cases, one specific area can be flooded with performers working in co-ordination, almost like a static show, except that there are no defined boundaries between audience and performer and the action needs to be observed in close proximity to be appreciated.

Because of the brevity of the appearance and the mobility of the performers, audience figures can be huge. However, this also means that it is difficult to collect money from the spectators. Such work can only be paid for by the organisers of large events who recoup the fee either by public subsidy or through ticket sales into a large enclosed area. For example, walkabout performers are often employed at festivals, big exhibitions, or 'fun parks', where the public has paid to see a whole package of attractions of which the walkabout theatre is only a part.

It is the increase in the number of these types of event that has encouraged the rapid development of walkabout theatre. The publicly subsidised outdoor theatre festival is a modern phenomenon and one can expect it to broaden its scope still further in the next decade. More commercial enterprises, such as 'theme parks', like Disneyland, can be expected to continue to spread far and wide as the leisure industry becomes more important. Most likely they will come to have a more educational aspect, becoming almost indistinguishable from some of the more enterprising museums which reproduce whole historical environments. Garden festivals are a similar phenomenon, but even the big commercial exhibitions, for such things as home furnishings, cars and boats, are beginning to employ walkabout performers to create a sense of fun amongst the serious business of selling. These large organisations have access to large amounts of money so, for the right kind of presentation and package, there is certainly a financial incentive.

BLENDING AND CONTRASTING WITH THE ENVIRONMENT

Unlike processions and journeys, with this kind of work, interaction with the audience and architecture are an absolute essential. There are a number of approaches that can be used. The first is to choose whether to blend in with the environment or to contrast with it. If blending in, characters and costumes are chosen that would not seem very out of place, if slightly unusual. It is not the appearance of the characters that attracts attention but their unusual behaviour. An example of this is when Natural Theatre dressed as police at the Glastonbury Festival; for the first time the real police had been allowed on the site, so no one was surprised to see them there. However, when they appeared to smoke drugs and snog in the grass, people were fascinated by the spectacle even after they had realised that they were really actors. Other examples are Scharlaten Theater's film crew, Theatre Decale's tourists and the Natural Theatre's protesters.

The other way is to contrast with the environment – to be very obviously out of place. There are a number of ways to do this, one of which was demonstrated by a youth theatre group at the Tarrega festival in 1989. Using the theme of preparing to sleep, a number of them carefully made a neat bed, brushed their teeth and their hair and did all the very normal private rituals of going to bed, quite ordinary in themselves but quite extraordinary in the middle of a street. Another member of the group mountaineered up the side of a building with considerable expertise and equipment, and made herself comfortable in a sleeping bag suspended from pegs hammered into the brickwork. These are normal characters performing normal actions but in the wrong place.

The other way to contrast with the environment is with totally abnormal characters. The Crazy Idiots dress as penguins, Desperate Men dress as escaped convicts and another of the Natural Theatre's pieces is with a group of egg-headed aliens. The beauty of this tactic is that the environment can be treated in a new way. The paranoid viewpoint of the escaped convicts sees a shopping centre in terms of hiding places, escape routes, guards and accomplices. For penguins and aliens the world is full of mystery and surprise; escalators, automatic and revolving doors, mirrors and even representational images such as statues and posters can be treated with fascination and miscomprehension. The aliens have a problem with steps of any sort so that even a pavement kerb becomes a major obstacle. The wonder and bewilderment at a modern shopping centre is something we can all identify with because they are alien places to everyone, artificially created and devoid of the human quirkiness characteristic of low-tech market-places. Watching the aliens and the penguins discover the city as if for the first time helps us to see it with new eyes; a letter-box becomes a mouth, a fountain becomes a swimming pool, a statue becomes a god. Not only is the architecture a mystery but the behaviour of the public too is either copied or misinterpreted. The aliens are constantly being photographed by the public so they have old-fashioned 'Brownie' cameras at the ready to imitate the actions of the photographers. A policeman directing traffic can be misinterpreted as just someone waving his arms around so they cheerfully wave back.

TACTICS

This 'journey of discovery' through quite ordinary streets is a tactic which can be used by less fantastic characters. Theatre Decale, a duo, have two walkabout pieces – one as tourists, the other as detectives searching for clues. Another duo, Trapu Zaharra Teatro Trapero, from Spain, are dressed in pyjamas with bandaged heads and act like harmless, bewildered mental patients who have escaped from the mental asylum. They do very little on their journey except stare at things; like children, they like to hug and be hugged by obliging members of the public. The two men hold hands for security, often tugging in opposite directions as different things attract them. Their gentleness and naivety bring out the parental side of the audience who are quite willing to help, and lull them into a caring relationship which makes the end of the journey all the more shocking. A real ambulance with a totally convincing medical crew suddenly drives up and they recapture the two frightened individuals, bundle them into the back and drive off with them.

Another tactic often used is that of offering some kind of service. As has been described, the Compagnie Extrêmement Prétentieuse offer themselves as waiters. The Lemmings used to dress in pink police uniforms and then would offer to direct traffic, help people across the road, give crime protection advice and test for intoxicating substances. These opening gambits could lead on to quite long and complicated improvisations with the public. Tour guides, photographers, salespeople and questionnaire interviewers are other types of service that have been used as walkabout characters. The emphasis here is on responding to people rather than the architecture and all these examples employ a verbal communication which is not so necessary in the 'journey of discovery' scenario. Allowing too much verbal communication opens up the possibility of the credibility of the characters being undermined by a public that may not be willing to suspend their disbelief. Délices Dada use speech extensively on their journey but the big difference is that the public has entered an implied contract with the performers right at the beginning. Walkabout theatre invites contact with a much wider range of people than would go on a journey such as theirs. Speech may also make the public feel they have to try to be witty; this is not only intimidating but may well put a pressure on the public that will prevent more natural, playful responses.

This leads us to the core of walkabout theatre – its excitement and dangers. The question is: will the audience play and if so how far are the spectators willing to go? It is the same question that faces animators in a stationary show but in this case the public may not have the inclination to get involved in a performance and have therefore not come half-way to meet the offer of play. The beauty of walkabout theatre is its ability to reach a non-theatrical public by going to them, rather than demanding of them too much commitment. However, this confrontational approach carries the danger of a hostile response. People can become very defensively aggressive if they feel they have suddenly become the centre of attention without their consent. It is to face this problem that Natural Theatre came up with another of their pieces – 'The Nannies'. What could be more harmless an image than a group of people pushing prams?

Like all successful walkabout pieces the group is clearly defined by matching costumes, in this case uniforms and oldfashioned prams. With their constant chattering, mainly focused either on the occupant of the pram or within the group itself, they can be watched from a distance, seemingly preoccupied with their own drama. By this means it is clearly stated that they are not out to confront members of the public. This tends to draw the public in, rather than repel them, and only if there appears to be a relatively warm, sympathetic crowd do they unleash their matronly fervour for hygiene and old-fashioned health remedies. The spectator is a passive participant in this encounter, which involves physical as well as verbal contact, as hands are inspected, partings are straightened and grumpiness is relieved by tickling. So the role of the spectator is a passive one, unlike in the relationship with other animators, nor is it essential to the performance.

Although precautions should be taken not to impose a confrontation on the audience, there will almost always be an implied invitation to play along with the game. The performer can present a member of the public with a number of choices. When the Natural Theatre as protesters lie down in front of the wheels of a bicycle to block its path, the cyclist can refuse to play by simply going round the side of them or can enter into the game either by defiantly carrying the bicycle over them or by accepting defeat and turning back. If the offer of play is accepted it can be developed by a more daring offer. The retreating cyclist can be chased; in which case he or she may either take playful evasive action or simply speed out of range. Each development of the game encourages the participant to get further involved while always leaving him or her a way out of the situation. This builds up trust but if the exit is closed the participant will become worried and not relaxed enough to play.

THÉÂTRE DÉCALE

In setting up these increasingly daring choices, the performers put themselves at risk, not only of rejection, but of causing offence. The skill is to take the risks without abusing the trust that the participant gives to the performer. Théâtre Décale are particularly expert in this way. Playing Inspector Clouseau-type detectives they use their quiet but very sure authority to inspect people's bags and bicycles and then walk off with them. They entered a clothing shop to inspect the premises and then walked out with a tailor's dummy. Keeping hold of this, they entered a bakery next door and later emerged without the dummy but with an entire display tray of pastries and so they went on, creating confusion down the street. The good humour and tolerance of the shopkeepers were tested to the limit but they were reassured by the obvious control and sensitivity of the performers, by the light-heartedness of the game and by the fact that the duo did not go far away but remained within the range of a short stretch of small shops. Amazingly they went as far as separating a mother from her 2-year-old daughter; both were momentarily disconcerted but such was the sensitivity and command with which it was done, the toddler went along with it until they all ended up sitting round a table together happily drinking coffee at the expense of an appreciative café owner.

At any point the participants could have objected or refused to co-operate but, since Decale could sense the limits of each person, they could take them that far and then let it go. Like all improvisation, it is a question of following a line of development as far as it will go and then embarking on a new one. The more daring the risk the greater the level of real tension created. Since laughter releases tension the level of comedy also increases as the excitement is built. After all, it is bound to be risky breaking down people's barriers, but that is a fundamental motive for this kind of work. All those shopkeepers were united by that confusion even if their reactions to it were quite different.

THE CRAZY IDIOTS AND CROWD CONTROL

The Crazy Idiots is a trio based in Germany but made up of English and Americans. They dress as penguins who are on a voyage of discovery through the city. They take risks in a different way, using the controlled static freeze of penguin movements to focus on specific objects and spectators. They threateningly surround particular people and then, using their masks, which have long beaks, they deftly dishevel the victims – hats are knocked off, hair is ruffled and ties are flipped out. One man made a hasty exit from this treatment but returned inconspicuously to continue watching. The trio spotted him without his realising and on a given signal they pounced on him anew (if it is possible to pounce with flippers on). This victimisation turned into a running gag but remained unthreatening because of their control of the situation. One of the ways they avoid putting too much pressure on a particular person is by constantly moving and dissolving the circle of spectators that quickly forms. Because of their slightly malicious behaviour, it is not safe to have a penguin behind you while watching another – you may find you are suddenly surrounded and being 'attacked' yourself. So the spectators are constantly being forced to look in different directions.

Most walkabout performers are aware of this problem of crowd density. If the audience is not arranged to allow for good sight-lines they will quickly bunch up and press in so that the kind of crush suffered by Guirigai develops. The wandering mental patients of Trapu Zaharra Teatro Trapero were followed by an increasingly large crowd in narrow streets and, because of their slow, gentle movements, they could not easily extract themselves from a situation; their characters would not have pushed through the crowd.

USE OF ARCHITECTURE

One way to extract oneself from a following horde of spectators is to enter shops or cafés. This will dissolve a large crowd because they will not all be able to see inside. It also means that a fresh public can be found inside and can also act as a sort of mini-theatre for those peering through the window. The danger, of course, is that shopkeepers can become very alarmed by strangely dressed intruders entering their shop with a dense crowd pressing in at the door and windows; not only is their merchandise at risk but their private domain has been invaded and they themselves have been unexpectedly forced into the centre of a lot of attention. Again, control and sensitivity can allay their fears; some show of willingness to pay for goods may help in this way. If they are amenable then window displays can offer a delightful area to use, especially clothes shops with mannequins. In a similar way striking a pose next to statues can make a very effective image.

Open spaces and raised areas improve sight-lines, low walls and street furniture can be mounted in order to pop up above the heads of the crowd, but the setting is also important. I remember seeing the Natural Theatre's aliens interspersed between the massive classical columns of Portsmouth City Hall. Not only did the symmetry look wonderful but the size of the structure added to their appearance of being lost in an awesome alien world. Again, the choice is to find settings that either contrast with or complement the characters portrayed. The penguins might look good by an icy pond but on the other hand they might look just as good sunbathing with dark glasses and Bermuda shorts.

GROUP CO-ORDINATION

Few walkabout groups rely entirely on improvisation. They usually have a few routines up their sleeve, either because the conditions enable a longer contact with a particular group of spectators or to provide an exit routine to bring a full stop to an improvisation, or even because the crowd is expecting 'a bit of a show'. As has been already mentioned, choreographed movement and co-ordinated costumes immediately attract attention; groups will often have an exit mode, a travelling mode and at

Figure 17 La Compagnie Extrêmement Prétentieuse in a
spontaneous use of architecture

least one short routine that acts as a sort of static mini-show. Routines are useful to bring a dispersed group together and concentrate the focus but their main use is to reassure the audience that you are professionals, much in the same way as a display of skill at the beginning of a stationary show indicates that you are not just amateurs dressed in silly costumes.

In a duo or even a trio the rapport between the performers may be good enough that they can instinctively follow each other down any line of improvisation. With larger groups this is impossibly complicated so it is necessary to follow a leader. This may be by means of pre-arranged signals to cue certain actions or, for more precise work, by standing behind them and following their exact movements. Dark glasses or masks that hide the eyes are extremely useful for this tactic. The Australian robotics group Chrome had a number of tightly choreographed routines that were initiated by signals but their *tour de force* was to be able to co-ordinate exact movements in an improvised interaction with spectators. This uncanny effect was enabled by their mirrored sunglasses; with their heads facing forward they appeared to look forward but their eyes could look to the side. This method is employed by the Crazy Idiots and Natural Theatre. It enables the performer to be constantly checking the audience and fellow performers while appearing to be immobile. By this means sudden co-ordinated actions can surprise the audience.

Routines can provide a safety net to be used if the environment does not inspire any improvisation or if the group is inexperienced. However, too much reliance on them removes the vitality of improvisation; as in any performance the pre-arranged 'script' of the piece should only be used as a base to take off from, otherwise it becomes empty and mechanical.

DEVISING WALKABOUT THEATRE

For the inexperienced, devising walkabout theatre remains a mystery – where do the ideas come from, especially since there is very little precedent to refer to? There are obviously no formulas; starting points are many and varied but one common line of development is from costume to character to routine. The Natural Theatre started life as the Bath Arts Workshop, which was based over a second-hand clothes and junk shop; all kinds of objects came into the shop that might provide a stimulus for a character or an action. For example, a collection of lightweight grey suits suggested FBI security agents. Later on the alien masks were obtained from a post-production throw-out from a large theatre and this provided the seed idea for that particular piece. Once the masks or costumes are found the actors put them on to see what kind of gestures and postures fit with them and gradually build characters. Finally the 'contre masque' is explored – behaviour which is opposite to that which is more obviously appropriate; the policeman and policewoman snogging is a good example. This adds the element of comedy.

Ralph Oswick is adamant about the importance of the complete image. It is not good enough, he says, when, for example, dressing as a vicar simply to take a shirt collar and wear it round the wrong way. A proper ecclesiastical dog-collar must be found otherwise spectators know immediately that you are only pretending so that the power of the image is lost. As in all acting it is not so much a question of pretending as 'being' whatever you have decided to play.

Once the characters have been built up, a rough plan of action must be decided upon. This could be as simple as arranging to meet up in the middle of a selected square. After that it is a question of taking the plunge and seeing what happens. The relationship with the audience will be the first thing to be determined; do they ignore you or stare from a distance? How do you become more noticed or alternatively less conspicuous? How can you draw them closer? Do you try to contact them directly or do you remain preoccupied with your own drama? A process of trial, error and analysis is undertaken. This may lead to rehearsing a series of signals and tight choreographed routines. The Natural Theatre uses reels of snapshots to examine the spatial relationships and to look at how watchable actors are from all directions. Walkabout theatre happens entirely in the round so the actor needs to keep the back and side profiles interesting. Ralph Oswick praised his co-founder Brian Popay because he was able to walk across a space with an unremarkable costume but attract attention through his interior concentration of energy.

Interaction with spectators can be gradually developed over a number of shows. Spontaneous actions or speech which are successful can be built into the repertoire and more difficult material abandoned. This process is true of all street performing in which improvisation plays a major part. The difference with walkabout theatre is that it will be better to start without too many premeditated ideas so that there is a greater openness to whatever happens and then build up the piece 'organically' rather than start with too much conceptualising. Although one may have no idea what one is actually going to do, it is most important to have a very clear idea of one's attitude to the physical environment and to the people within it, otherwise uncertainty becomes insecurity and an audience will not want to go along with it.

STAYING IN CHARACTER

It has already been described (p. 64) how Ralph Oswick outfaced a number of heavy duty security guards while dressed as a nanny. This is a particularly extreme example of a common situation – that of having one's credibility challenged either by authorities or by drunks and oafs. The general rule is to always be acting the character if you are dressed in the costume. The image should be complete from start to finish. In some extreme cases performers have been arrested and placed in a cell before they have broken the illusion when an admission of their true identity would have kept them out of trouble. The temptation to deny the reality of the characters may be strong in these situations but it is perfectly possible to maintain the performance by responding in the way that the characters would react. After all, police and security guards are only other people dressed in unusual costumes playing a role. Drunks and oafs may be a serious challenge; some performers find it interesting to play close to the edge of real violence, but in general it is best to use an exit routine and avoid contact.

Conversely, serious problems can arise if you are genuinely mistaken for the real thing. If you are dressed as a policeman and there is a real emergency you may be expected to take charge. To avoid this problem it is best to have some small indication that you are not real. Natural Theatre uses subtle theatre make-up which not only brightens the face but, at a close distance, makes the distinction from the real thing. However, one is always bound to feel vulnerable performing outside and the sort of attitude required for dealing with this is dealt with in the next section.

Part III

Performing and performers

Chapter 16

The live event

At the beginning of Part II the practical differences between theatre indoors and outdoors were discussed. Having described all the various forms it is useful to focus in on the qualities and attitudes essential in all outdoor performance and their implications for the performers.

PERFORMING

Contact with the audience

The relationship between performer and audience is the essence of any theatrical event and more than any other factor determines its nature. Various forms of direct contact with the audience were explored years ago by the underground theatre during the 1960s. It is now common in fringe theatre. Audience participation has even found its way into the West End; a recent hit show, called *Five Guys Named Moe*, finishes the first half with almost all the audience from the stalls dancing on the stage.

Although not every outdoor performer uses audience participation they all need to have a much greater awareness of its mood and composition than is the case in indoor theatre. They are able to do this because they can see the audience much better than if they had lights shining in their eyes and the audience hidden in darkness. Being able to see them allows for much more interaction with individuals but having such an intimate contact with their responses can be alarming and cause problems.

The inexperienced performers will be afraid of the audience – afraid of its judgement, afraid of its rejection, afraid of making fools of themselves. This fear must be overcome as soon as possible. It either makes the performers timid and apologetic or tenses them, preventing them from responding in an open way. In tough environments, such as the Pompidou Centre in Paris, it is difficult for even experienced performers to lose this fear, so unless the beginner feels at home in such places, it will be better to start with a more conducive environment where the show is more likely to be appreciated than in hard-nosed city centres. A crowd that is cynical, sceptical and sophisticated may give an uncomfortably rough ride to an inexperienced performer either by heckling or by walking away. To cope with this, many young performers in these situations become very aggressive as a defence against their vulnerability. They are physically tense and tend to 'put down' the audience, either by being patronising, or with severe abuse, or even by forcefully dragging 'volunteers' out of the crowd and humiliating them in order to make themselves look clever. Surprisingly this tactic sometimes works in the short term because its invulnerability gives it a street credibility. Chris Lynham can work the toughest audiences because of his 'I don't give a fuck about the audience' approach which disguises his care in his work. His ebullient approach to individuals is, in fact, full of sensitivity. He challenges his helpers but is wary of losing the sympathy of the crowd. Less experienced performers develop a certain pride verging on arrogance – 'Nobody puts me down!' It is not that the performer is insensitive to the audience but that his or her sensitivity is slightly paranoid and, because there is fear of the audience, there is no openness towards them.

In the long run, or a wider context, this tactic falls flat on its face. This is most clearly shown when this type of performer is confronted with an audience that is 'soft'. The audience is eager to see the show, easily impressed and generally supportive. There are no hecklers to do battle with and this seems uncomfortably quiet to the performer; this increases their paranoia and raises the level of their aggression. The audience is mystified by the habitual reflexes of the performer which appear blunt, crude and unnecessarily abrasive. They rapidly become alienated.

Hopefully the performer loses the fear through a gradually growing confidence in his or her abilities so that, far from seeing the audience as an enemy, he or she sees them as a friend to get

to know. The performer will be able to see them as individuals
with whom eye contact is possible rather than as an amorphous
mass and therefore less threatening. Coming from this point of
view the performer sees in the audience and the rest of the
environment a rich potential of exciting possibilities to explore
and develop. The relationship is one neither of inferiority, nor
superiority, but of equality. Because the performers are not
desperate for the audience's approval, they can be honest about
mistakes, unafraid of failing or making fools of themselves. For
example, jugglers have to learn fast how to make a joke when
they drop their clubs (which they inevitably do because of the
wind, if not their own mistakes). The worst thing they can do is
to pretend it did not happen – their embarrassment embarrasses
the audience. The simplicity and honesty of the relationship give
the performer the subtext of 'There's all of you there and just
me here and we can have fun together because I am an expert in
fun'. It is like watching someone who has held their breath,
taken the plunge and is now enjoying themselves in the water
and entreating others to come and join in. It is liberating to see
people without fear: fear of embarrassment, of humiliation, of
failure, of authority, of physical contact or of treading on other
people's political niceties. The public is challenged but they all
feel 'I wish I could be like that'. In this sense there is a social,
spiritual and political event happening because feelings of play,
sharing, caring and liberation from authoritarian principles are
being stimulated. (Outdoor performers tend to be anti-
authoritarian because they are outsiders who have rejected a
normal, regular life-style.)

Improvisation

The techniques of improvisation are a whole subject in themselves and dealt with at length by other books. In this context it is
useful to examine the general attitude required rather than
individual methods.

   Although many outdoor performers do not use improvisation
in the sense of spontaneous creation, all of them will develop an
ability to adapt easily to different circumstances. The flexibility
required is one of the main differences from indoor theatre.
Inexperienced outdoor performers will tend to ignore changing
circumstances because they see them as a threat to what they

have previously worked out and do not know how to cope. Improvisation means not only being able to cope with problems but, more importantly, being open to more subtle possibilities offered by the environment. For example, a docile pigeon wandering around the edge of the performing area is hardly an interruption but it could lead to a beautiful interaction if the timing is right.

As well as being alert to possibilities, it is also essential to have the courage or the confidence to risk leaving the pre-arranged sequence to go into the unknown here-and-now. This element of risk is important not only in receiving but also in creating unforeseen events. Doing an imitation of a pigeon is a safe improvisation but imitating a high-status member of the public, or even a policeman, to their face sets up a very real, exciting sense of danger. We have seen how provocateurs create tension by risking the infringement of taboos and how animators encourage spectators to break with their normal behaviour; the audience becomes enthralled in the drama of how far the performer will go. Will the participant be offended? It is because performers dare to stop traffic, take their clothes off, be rude to children or whatever, that they are fascinating. None of these actions need be aggressive or insensitive, not all of the threats need to be fulfilled, it is the challenging possibility that creates the dramatic tension.

The ability to take risks depends on the personality of the performer. Some relish the exhilaration of danger, others build up a secure base of sure-fire material which provides a springboard to dive off into the unknown. If they play safe and just rest on their material then the situation will be much less exciting for them and the audience; they will deny themselves the opportunity to learn and develop.

Energy and control

It has already been mentioned how hard it is for solos and duos to dominate a difficult space such as Covent Garden or the Pompidou Centre. The latter has a gentle slope so that it is like playing to raked seating. The designers were thoughtful in this aspect, the trouble is that there is no back wall, except the building itself and this is too far away from the main concourse of people. The main space at Covent Garden has the wonderful backdrop of the portico of St Paul's Church but it is an awkward size, being too small to accommodate more than one show at a time. The audience tends to sit on a kerb too far from the back and spectators are often reluctant to come forward (into the shade on a sunny day). The balcony of a pub looks down upon the square like the upper circle of a theatre. Both these spaces are hard to master because they are so expansive. A loud voice will help, of course, but it also requires a large style of acting to fill such spaces. It is like playing in the vastness of a Greek amphitheatre except without the good acoustics.

To tackle these and similar situations it is useful to employ large, bold, fully extended gestures of the whole body. Using the type of exaggerated postures associated with the commedia dell'arte and nineteenth-century melodrama will assist in conveying what is going on but may not fit in with the style of the piece. Trying to play to an audience on all sides means that there must be much rotation of the head and body in order to keep all the audience feeling included in the event. Holding an extended posture and rotating the head, while speaking a phrase, helps in this way and avoids too much closing off from the different sides. To assist with voice projection while speaking to another character, all speech can be directed outwards; even a phrase such as 'I love you' can be spoken towards the audience if the body gesture is well defined towards the intended character.

The voice is often strained to the limit and many performers without training develop a rasp. It is said that Richard Burton developed his voice by shouting on the mountains. Playing a brass instrument develops the power of the diaphragm and is a useful warm-up at the beginning of a show. Enunciating clear hard consonants is an important part of any voice training but becomes even more important when the vocal chords are straining to compete with mechanical diggers and wailing sirens. Clarity is as important in movement as it is in speech – moving from one defined posture to another, avoiding small fussy movements helps the audience to pick up visually what is going on even if they cannot hear it. Similarly the face should be used economically with well-defined expressions. In general, timing needs to be slightly slower in order for the meaning to be clear; speech needs to be 'declaimed' rather than rattled off as a stand-up comedian might do.

Control is therefore essential and is often glaringly absent in untrained performers. However, they usually compensate with the other essential ingredient – energy. Just making oneself heard against a background of city noise can be exhausting in itself. There is no substitute for energy but the more control there is, the less energy is wasted with unnecessary movements and excess tension. A young performer relying too much on energy will tend to move too fast to achieve maximum clarity. Adrenalin accelerates the mind which produces the necessary alertness, but an effort is required to slow down the body and hold gestures, rather than disappear in a flurry of arms and rapid facial expressions. The charge of adrenalin is a useful by-product of the type of fear mentioned earlier, enabling a 100 per cent engagement in the performance without which there can be no take-off. Although it fuels the motor of the show it must be controlled, otherwise the performers are driven along rather than driving it themselves.

Being in control does not mean blocking spontaneity, rather the reverse. Performers who are in command of their own timing and actions have a better foundation to depart from the pre-arranged scenario and ultimately it is this take-off that gives the event its life. So the skill of performing is really a delicate balancing act – to be sensitive but not timid, to be challenging without being aggressive, to be alert and full of energy but relaxed, to create tension without being tense and to be controlled but also spontaneous. A good performer, be it dancer, singer, musician, at the height of his powers, in an ecstatic state of involvement with their expression, is like the shaman in his trance, generating an energy to give out to those who witness the event, celebrating life by living it to the full.

One of the worst shows I have seen was at an affluent resort on the Côte d'Azure, by a man who had got himself in a bad way. His show was based on the familiar fakir acts of fire and broken glass but instead he used only a cigarette and a single shard of broken glass. He would place the glass between his large bicep and tattooed forearm and bend the arm at the elbow so that the glass was wedged into the skin. This was done as a display of macho bravado and he grimaced a broken-toothed grin when he saw a few passers-by stopping in disbelief. The glass left a deep red mark on his skin but worse was to come. When he tried to requisition a cigarette the elegant tourists, taking their evening promenade, recoiled in horror because he was stripped to the waist and slightly drunk. When he finally succeeded, he proceeded to burn his arms with the lighted cigarette, particularly working the tip into sores left by previous displays of pain endurance. To his surprise hardly anyone wanted to watch this gruesome spectacle and despite some aggressive hustling he ended up with only a few francs. Resentfully, he began to shout abuse at the whole street. No wonder that, in some parts, busking has a bad name.

PERFORMERS

The question is sometimes asked, why are there no really famous outdoor performers? There are two reasons for this; first they hardly ever receive any of the media coverage that could make them famous, and second they generally do not do it for very long. The two reasons are linked because, with no status attached to the art by the media, successful performers will look for that attention elsewhere. It is a chicken-and-egg situation. There are, however, other reasons why they move on to other work.

A typical busker's career would be of a young hopeful who masters his fear and develops his skill by trial and error, repetition and the constant un-polite judgement of audience reaction. Having arrived at a show that works well in familiar surroundings, he uses the advantage of easy mobility to try places further afield, perhaps to the capitals of Europe or various big festivals, or perhaps beginning to be booked to do shows for a pre-arranged fee. He may become hampered by cultural and language differences and return to the security of his home pitch or he may sail through difficulties to success. Either way, there will be a desire to move on because too much repetition in the same place becomes boring and he has not come into this line of work for regularity.

Eventually all start to see the attraction of work indoors. The lights give a focus which means that more precise work can be done and less energy expended. Other conditions are better and outdoors the variability of conditions becomes wearing; as Les Bubb said, 'The streets are a great training ground but I got fed up with bad sight-lines and bumpy pavements, littered with broken glass.' Unpredictable weather means unpredictable income. The work, at least in Europe, is only seasonal unless constant travelling is undertaken. After a number of years public recognition seems deserved but unattainable outdoors. The megalomaniac tendencies, mentioned earlier, can often give successful acts an over-estimation of their abilities. There may also be a genuine frustration with the limitations of the show they have developed as far as it can go. Entertainers and provocateurs turn into communicators and performing artists; they may feel they cannot make this change in the hostile and variable conditions which they have become over-familiar with. Altogether there is a desire for steadier work rather than the extreme highs and lows of performing outdoors.

Dogtroep explain some of the advantages they have found of working indoors after working for years outside:

> You can work with low-volume sounds; it's easier to con-centrate the audience's attention within four walls; every day we extend the landscape of objects which give the performance its shape without having to store them away in safety for the night.

Often this move inside does not work. The ticket-paying audience is more selective and expects a polished performance for its money. The bold style appears bombastic in a confined space. The probable lack of training now becomes apparent because, with the more concentrated focus, control becomes more important than energy. There are also no interventions to play with and the audience has disappeared into the darkness, so the contact with them becomes lost. The desire to communicate an idea by using a narrative or to be more 'artistic' often fails because of a lack of comprehension of the complexities involved. The performers are often surprised by this failure. They know they are good performers and, since they are probably respected as such, it comes as a severe blow. They are then in the difficult position of either giving up their expectations and returning to the rigours of the outdoors or of trying to pursue an indoor career. Very few succeed.

However, there are many well-established groups and solo performers who perform outside out of preference, at least for part of the year. These are ones for whom life-style and commercial success are less important than artistic and political aims. For them outdoor theatre is not a stepping stone to some-where else but a stimulating and enjoyable area of work, full of opportunities to contact people and places that would not other-wise come into their sphere of experience. Ultimately it is the motivation that affects how long people stay in it.

Women in outdoor theatre

Another question that is frequently asked is why there are so few women doing outdoor theatre. Lady Komedie from Holland is one of a number of excellent women's companies doing cabaret and outdoor work. In Britain, Cunning Stunts was followed by others doing circus skills such as Skinning the Cat, or Skin and Blisters. There are also many strong women performers within mixed groups. Despite attempts to redress the balance, such as the festival of women performers at Covent Garden a few years ago, there are hardly any solo women street performers. Joanna Bassi, from Italy, is a notable exception, and in Britain, Patty Bee.

There seem to be a number of reasons for this. The first is that, until relatively recently, women's education did not encourage them to acquire the assertiveness, self-confidence and inde-pendence necessary to dominate a street environment. These are more traditionally male attributes. The strong voice required of a performer did not seem to be so developed in women, who were not encouraged to shout and cheer in their youth as boys were. Another reason is that if women had tra-ditionally been attracted to theatre for its glamour, it was not to be found in outdoor work. While this is true for both men and women, women tend to be seen in terms of their sexuality first and as performers second. Dealing with hecklers is part of the job but, outdoors, women are likely to be the subject of com-ments of a sexual nature, rather than to do with the show. For example, at a festival in Holland, Joanna Bassi played a school-teacher, whose skirt came off in the same way as a clown's trousers fall down. She sets herself up as a high-status character and the comedy is in the delayed realisation, the indignity and the humiliation. Although this was performed in front of a fairly 'liberal' public, there were a number of wolf-whistles and com-ments coming from the back of the crowd, which she dealt with very effectively. At the same festival, Chris Lynham took all his clothes off in his show and there was no such reaction.

Personal remarks are much harder to deal with than comments

Figure 18 Joanna Bassi

that are concerned with the show itself. Perhaps for this reason there are fewer black solo performers. Those performers who are vulnerable to taunting can be very successful if they pre-empt and make fun of the stereotyped attitudes towards them. A black performer, seen in Belgium, created an entrancing tension by being open and honest about the taboo subject of his colour: 'Here I am amongst all you white dudes . . . ,' he declared. Making such a point of his own vulnerability made it easier for onlookers to place themselves in the vulnerable position of participating in his show.

It has also been suggested that women do not have the same opportunities for comedy as men because they do not have such traditional hero stereotypes to deflate. Because contrast is so important for comedy, male performers have the macho, the authoritarian and the romantic attributes to play with. However, women can make fun of their own traditional image – pretty, delicate and unassertive. Patty Bee totally inverts these attributes of femininity by playing characters that are unattractive, out-rageous and very assertive. One character she performs, Mistress Crabbyquim, is a raucous medieval purveyor of revolting cures for ailments, who is dirty and has a festering skin. Another character is Lady Christobel, an alcoholic tramp aristocrat. Actors playing aristocrats are often the subject of physical and verbal abuse by deprived inner-city kids; the fact that she is also an alcoholic tramp and a woman makes her even more of a target. She has been kicked and grabbed and had things thrown at her. Normally, however, she can avoid physical abuse by a quick-witted verbal response to provocation, which immediately establishes that she is unshockable and, if need be, can outdo any man in gross vulgarity, even the roughest sort of Hell's Angel.

Like other good provocateurs, she rarely has to go to ex-tremes; it is enough of a threat to show that she is quite capable of going as far as is necessary to get the better of boorish males. It is not that she seeks to intimidate, merely that she is prepared to go into situations, such as night clubs and rough inner-city festivals, that other solo performers would not dare to. The fact that she mainly does walkabout theatre means that she can walk away from difficult members of the public, unlike the more vulnerable static performers. Nowadays she usually works with a partner, who is always nearby if an ugly situation arises. Their 'itinerant, intimate, interactional spectacular' is half provocateur, half animator in aim. Patty Bee found that she could risk provoking members of the public further than a male performer might because a man is more likely to elicit physical aggression than a woman. Certainly, she says, in the 1970s, a woman was much less likely to get hit in public than a man would. Possibly the 'sexual revolution' has changed all that.

Patty Bee is fortunate to have had her early experiences in the radical theatre of the late 1960s – in indoor theatre nudity was often used to shock in a way that is now much less common. These early experiences had a toughening effect that younger performers would not have had. She also had the fortifying experience of performing outdoors alongside such strong performers as Ian Hinchliffe, Lol Coxhill and particularly Paddy Fletcher.

As attitudes change there are gradually more women performers doing outdoor work. Although the future can now be glimpsed, there is still a long way to go before there are as many women as men in outdoor theatre.

Opposing tendencies

There are two clearly opposing tendencies in outdoor theatre. On the one hand there are those who try to appeal to the widest possible audience and on the other those who target their work at a more specific audience; these latter might, in the end, appeal to a wider audience than they had intended, but the performance is not designed with them in mind.

At its most extreme, the appeal of this second type is so narrow as to be obscure and inaccessible to everyone except an initiated few. An extreme example was the performance artist seen at the Pompidou Centre who rolled around in a black plastic bag accompanied by strange electronic music. Nobody knew what she was doing but it looked like art and it looked modern so many people tried hard to appreciate it but were left with a slight feeling of inferiority and exclusion because all they could see was someone rolling around in a plastic bag. The problem for pure performance art is that there are no guidelines, no criteria for success. It is dependent on a few critics to be judged since the reaction of an unsophisticated public may not be taken into consideration. There is a danger that being weird or outrageous is sometimes considered enough.

Less extreme are those that appeal to an 'arthouse' audience. These can often be identified by their use of music that is influenced by traditional music from Japan, China, or Bali. Other groups might use loud rock music and appeal specifically to the young, trendy audiences. Most provocateurs and performing artists appeal to a narrow audience.

The extreme example of the other type is those who pander so much to popular taste that the work is trite – the ghastly figure of Ronald McDonald, the clown sometimes used by the hamburger chain to do 'walkabout' outside their premises. He is there not only to attract children but to make parents feel that this is a safe place to bring their family. Traditional circus and fairground are a source of inspiration for this type. At its less extreme form, there are the 'romantics' who draw on myth, legend and folklore for inspiration, perhaps using a medieval, commedia dell'arte, or nineteenth-century look. They appeal to the widest possible range of people, particularly older people and children, because they make people feel safe, they fulfil their expectations of outdoor theatre and thus reinforce them. They try hard not to be threatening. In this sense they confirm the status quo. This popular appeal and 'harmlessness' have a commercial potential. In this group are the majority of entertainers and animators.

Obviously most artists combine the two tendencies in some way or another but, at the same time, most will recognise to which they give most emphasis. It is important to consider this dialogue not only because the two groups can be quite averse to each other but also because it affects the way the general public perceive outdoor theatre. It is particularly important for anyone involved in putting on a street theatre festival to strike the appropriate balance for their area.

The difference between the two tendencies can be seen in a milder form in California. In San Francisco's Fisherman's Wharf the buskers must audition to play to the tourists so they tend to present 'safe' acts. At the more hip Venice Beach area the acts are more inventive, offbeat and less 'acceptable', like the man in a wheelchair who has a tape-recording of racing cars to which he does various 'wheelie' stunts, as if he is on a racetrack. Other acts with fire and limbo-dancing are rougher, less polished and less pretty than at Fisherman's Wharf but have a raw freshness. One of the dangers for street theatre in the future is not so much lack of popular appeal but an over-compensation in its favour – it may become safe and sterile, mistaking the common touch for common attitudes and losing its provocative zeal.

A separate, but related, question is that of the interaction between rural and urban environments. In the 1970s there was a move away from the cities into the country. Many of the early radical artists, who had received their initial impetus in the sophisticated atmosphere of urban art schools, later moved to the country. In Britain, Welfare State, IOU, Forkbeard Fantasy and Horse and Bamboo, amongst others, based themselves far away from urban culture. This move was an extension of the move of visual artists out of the galleries and on to the streets. There was the same desire to confront a fresh public with their work. The fresher public in the rural areas received their work at face value, often seeing comic absurdity when surrealism was intended. The rural fairs, described earlier, provided the opportunity for urban performers to face a rural audience. In the last ten years there has been a shift in emphasis back to the cities. Archaos is the obvious example; a fairly traditional circus, touring rural areas by horse and cart, they decided to drop the romantic image and 'get real', revelling in the power of mechanical devices and rock music. Groups such as Malabar, Generik Vapeur, Bow Gamelan, Urban Sax and Test Department embrace modern technology, relishing in engineering, welding and powerful effects. Their rejection of the past is often an angry one, charged by the frustration, resentment and megalomania of youth – they often use apocalyptic themes. Quite opposed to making people feel safe, they challenge, often aggressively. They can flourish in a tough city environment because they expose no vulnerability. A city also provides enough density of population for there to be a sub-culture large enough to draw sufficient audience. The subtle differences in society mean that what is acceptable in, for example, big cities may not be acceptable in a rural area and vice versa. Rural audiences might be more easily shockable in terms of sex and violence and urban audiences demand more novelty and sophistication.

What seems to be an essential ingredient for dynamic artistic activity is a rejection of the current forms of expression – the artists rejecting the gallery system and taking their work on to the streets, the rejection of urban sophistication for the more fresh and 'real' rural audiences, and the later rejection of woolly, rural romanticism for the more 'hard-edged' realism of the city. Although there is rarely a totally new idea, there is a rearrangement of old ideas which effectively reinvents the old form. At each step it is the interface with the public that moulds the new form.

FESTIVALS

Many festivals come and go over the years and most change the amount of their outdoor theatre from year to year. The list given in the second part of this section (pp. 198–200) is not comprehensive, but is given as a rough guide as to where and when to go and see outdoor theatre. The first part of this section is a comparison of those few festivals that are designed mainly for outdoor theatre.

In any one year, in Britain, a particular city might have an emphasis on outdoor theatre, especially if it is intending to develop a new cultural image, for example, Glasgow in 1990 and Birmingham in 1991. The London International Festival of Theatre usually has some outdoor theatre but it occurs only every two years. Alternative Arts, who used to organise the Covent Garden street theatre, now have one or two annual one-day festivals in London, mainly of entertainers. Cardiff has had a festival of street theatre that has been growing over the years, supported by both sponsorship and the local council.

The longest-running annual outdoor theatre festival in Britain is the Hat Fair in Winchester which has been going since 1971. Originally it was a fairly informal gathering of friends, trying out their new shows and being paid by money into the hat. Gradually it gained enough status to receive a small amount of financial assistance from the regional arts funders. It aimed to provide buskers with hospitality, with conducive conditions in which to perform and, if possible, a small fee. By these means it was hoped to raise the standard of street theatre and assist artists in developing from casual buskers to fee-paid professionals. An evening of cabaret provided a showcase for some of the best acts and gave the opportunity for the artists to use a more controlled environment. The bizarre mix of new work made this cabaret a huge success and, over the years, expanded to four nights of acts. The organisers saw the festival very much as a community event, with a series of workshops to develop local talent and a street party on the last night. It is a reflection of conservative British attitudes that the local council and business community remained totally resistant to appeals for financial help, despite the fact that Winchester has the richest population in the country. After running on a shoestring for twenty years, the festival has now succeeded in obtaining at least some sponsorship.

In continental Europe there are a growing number of festivals specifically for outdoor theatre. In France, the ones at Chalon-sur-Saône and Aurillac are particularly important, the latter calling itself the European Festival of Street Theatre, although in reality most of the groups are from France and Spain. The Avignon Theatre Festival is longer established, it has a combination of indoor shows, programmed outdoor shows and itinerant buskers. Belgium has a festival at Ghent, also calling itself the European Street Theatre Festival. In Vienna there is a contemporary arts festival which has street theatre. The southern Netherlands have the Limburg Street Theatre Festival. All these festivals act as showcases for other work. Generally the person(s) responsible for programming a festival will go to most of the other festivals to identify the current successful groups. There is a certain competition between these festivals so they try to discover up-and-coming talent before any of the others. Up-and-coming talent is also likely to come cheaper than well-established companies. This festival circuit is extremely important because success at one can lead quite rapidly to work further afield. Programmers from Canada, Israel, Australia, Singapore, Hong Kong and eastern Europe can be seen at European festivals looking for appropriate companies to invite.

Programmers will have several criteria – to suit their audiences, to suit their locations and, of course, to suit their own personal preferences, which are often a reflection of the national taste. In France, for example, programmers have a preference for work that is self-consciously artistic, perhaps because they want to distance their festival from their strong, continuous tradition of street entertainers. In Holland, the Festival of Fools, which ran on and off for almost a decade, set a different tone; comedy took precedence over art. Although this festival no longer takes place it must have originally influenced the organisers of the Limburg Street Theatre Festival, which has been running since 1983 with increasing international importance. This festival is fortunate to have not just one programmer but several, with slightly different tastes, who decide in co-ordination which companies to invite. This means there is more balance in their choice, which is important because the Limburg Festival is unusual in having an enormous range of locations in rural and urban environments over an area seventy miles long. In some small villages solo entertainers are appropriate and in the centre of the city of Maastricht large groups, such as Malabar, who particularly appeal to the urban youth, present their theatrical spectacles. In between these two extremes there is a fine balance kept between the different types and sizes of visiting shows. There also seems to be good communication between the programmers and the local organisers, who are in touch with the local response to shows. This ensures that the audiences are happy with the shows they are receiving and also provide suitable conditions for the very different requirements of the artists.

At Aurillac some of the companies are invited on a normal fee-paying basis, others are '*compagnies de passage*' – they are not paid but are provided with a site, a time and an entry into the publicised daily programme. There is also plenty of scope for busking. The mix seems a good idea as it enables programmers to see up-and-coming artists as well as established ones. Groups like Boîte à Pandore went there as buskers and were subsequently invited to take on more fee-paid work than they were able to do. However, Aurillac is more of a showcase for work than a festival for the local people. There was a feeling of tolerance by the local community, rather than enjoyment. This is particularly the case because much of the work, paid or otherwise, was either inaccessible Performance Art or over-aggressive urban culture, which was quite out of place in this provincial market town.

In Spain there is a wonderful festival at Tarrega, near Barcelona. It is only a small town but people from all over the region, particularly the young, are attracted by the mix of theatre and music. They are able to camp along the banks of the river, where there are many stalls for food and crafts. The festival is also the town fiesta, so there are traditional events, such as the extraordinary six-high human pyramids, and a general air of celebration all through the nights. In the spirit of Spanish carnival there is much singing, dancing, processing, music and fireworks in the streets. Every little square has a small stage, some with lights and sound for the evening shows. There is a chaotic mix of traditional entertainers, untraditional entertainers and experimental work, both static and mobile, crowded into the streets, sometimes concurrently. On the last night there is usually some large-scale spectacle, often preceded by a procession right through the town and always involving copious amounts of pyrotechnics. As compared with some festivals, it is refreshing to see experimental work being watched by the rural working class. It demonstrates an openness on the part of both audience and artists that is not found in more sophisticated and subdivided cultures.

Some festivals which feature street theatre

Britain

Alternative Arts, London	July/August
Bear Fair, Peebles	July
Bradford	September
Brighton Festival	May
Campus, Devon	July–August
Cardiff Street Festival	July
Castlefield Carnival, Manchester	August
City of London Festival	July
Conwy Street Theatre Festival	July/August
Edinburgh Fringe Festival	August–September
Glastonbury Festival	June
Hat Fair, Winchester	July
London International Festival of Theatre	July (Biennial)
Mayfest, Glasgow	May
Stockton on Tees	August
Streetbiz, Glasgow	August

Ireland

Cork Fringe Festival	August
Dublin Street Carnival	June
Galway Festival	July
Limerick Festival	July
Omagh Festival	September/October
Sligo Festival	September/October

Belgium

Chassepierre	August
Trefpunt, Ghent	July

France

Arrivées d'Airs Chauds, Douarnenez	July
Arts Rivages, Rennes	summer
Avant Scène, Cognac	July
Avignon Theatre Festival	July/August
Chalon Dans La Rue, Chalon-sur-Saône	July
Eclat, Aurillac	August
Festival de Spectacle de Rue, Morlaix	July–August
Festival Rencontres, Lille	September/October
Festival International de Mime, Périgueux	August
Festival de Théâtre Européen, Grenoble	July
Jazz Sous Les Pommiers, Coutances	May
Turbulence, Châlons-sur-Marne	June

Germany

Cologne Festival	August
Dortmund Festival	July
Landeshanptstracht, Kiel	June

Most cities in Germany have festivals which include an element of outdoor theatre.

Netherlands

Limburg Straat Theater Festival	August
Terschelling Festival	June
Vlissingen Straat Theater Festival	July/August

Spain

Campana de Teatro en la Calle, Almeria	August
Expo 92, Seville	
Festival de Teatro en la Calle, Almuñécar	August
Festival International de Sitges	Spring
Mostra de Teatro Comico e Festivo, Cangas	September
Segovia Festival	June
Tarrega Festival, Catalonia	September

Rest of Europe

Arhus Festival, Denmark
Copenhagen Festival

Dubrovnik International Theatre Festival,
   Yugoslavia
Roskilde Festival, Denmark
Spoleto Teatro Sperimentale, Rome
Tampere Festival, Finland
Vienna Festival

Australia
Adelaide Street Festival
Melbourne Comedy Festival

Canada
Festival d'Eté de Lanaudiere, Quebec (Biennial)
Juste Pour Rire, Montreal
Ottawa-Ontario Festival
Vancouver Festival
Victoria International Festival

New Zealand
Auckland Festival
Wellington International Festival

Elsewhere
Archangelsk International Street Theatre
   Festival, Russia
Hong Kong Festival
Korakuan Park, Tokyo
Saraton, Tashkent, Uzbekistan

Part IV

The present and the future

Chapter 17

An eye on the horizon

PUBLIC REACTION

Since the 1970s a number of significant changes have taken place with regard to outdoor theatre. From a performer's point of view, one of the most apparent is that the public is now more used to outdoor theatre. The very fresh reaction that could be achieved fifteen years ago is found only in culturally remote places. Recently I attended one of the first street theatre festivals in Russia. Together with groups from Poland and Italy we made a procession through a town that had been closed to foreigners for decades because there were military factories nearby. Street theatre was unheard of, so the curiosity and excitement were intense. It was as if the entire process of glasnost was encapsulated in that half hour. Back in Britain, the public reaction to people doing unusual things in the street seems much more blasé. Most people in Britain have heard of the new-look Covent Garden and therefore know about the entertainers there. Because charity fundraisers have acquired the habit of going round in fancy dress, there is also a general suspicion that anyone in costume will be asking for money.

NO SMALL CHANGE IN THE SHOPPING CENTRES

Another change that has taken place is the gradual transformation of the centres of towns and cities all over Europe. There are far more pedestrianised streets and these make an ideal setting for street performers. Occasionally the architects have included an arrangement of seating around an open space with the apparent intention of allowing for performances. Very rarely, however, do they take into consideration such important features as a back wall. More usually in these pedestrianised streets the seating faces opposite directions, with plants and signposts, evenly spaced in order to break up the space. These can make it much more difficult to site a static show of any size, although for walkabout theatre they provide much more to play with. In general the pedestrianised streets are a vast improvement, giving more room for people to watch from a distance, without obstructing the passage of others. The diminished noise from traffic is also a great asset.

Another change has been the growth in the number of enclosed shopping centres. The aim of these is to provide a comfortable environment in which to shop by excluding the possibility of bad weather. This is not all that is excluded. One would imagine that these shopping centres would be an ideal performing area, since the sound is enclosed and interruptions less frequent. However, the thoroughfares are nearly always private property and so permission must be obtained before putting on a performance. They are staffed by security guards who are likely to be much less flexible in their approach than the police. Quite often their system of communications does not operate very efficiently, despite their short-wave radios, so that they prevent any performance, even if it has been pre-arranged, until they eventually get clearance from their invisible superiors. The acoustics of such places can make them difficult to work in. If there is not 'canned music', there is at least music issuing out of shops. The enclosed space means that escalators, fountains and footsteps create a constant hum of noise much louder than it would be outside. There is even less likelihood of finding a suitable back wall in indoor shopping centres because they contain uninterrupted shopfronts, which are used for display purposes. The narrower passages mean there is more likely to be some obstruction. The managements of these shopping centres are most unlikely to allow casual buskers to do any shows within their premises. However, it is becoming more frequent for them to buy in professional companies to animate their artificial environments. So these shopping centres could possibly provide an increasing market for one type of performer but at the exclusion of another.

THE ECONOMIC SITUATION

At the time of writing the state of outdoor theatre in Britain does not seem hopeful. The combined effects of recession, poll tax capping and government policies towards the arts mean that there is much less money around for promoters, performers and punters. Over the last ten years many British groups have moved abroad – Footsbarn, Lindsey Kemp and British Events to name a few; others earn an important part of their income from tours abroad, where they feel there is more value given to them as artists. The dynamic period of innovation during the 1970s has given way to more market-orientated productions. Outdoors, pure Performance Art has all but died out and political theatre is virtually non-existent. Although elements of both can still be found in the work of many groups, its radical nature has been toned down to make it more 'acceptable'. Site-specific work is currently becoming known as Environmental Arts and is enjoying a belated honeymoon with arts-funding bodies. Community Theatre is also recognised as a 'good thing' but both these areas of work are starved of funds. Their low profile is unlikely to attract sponsorship and, since they do not tour, they are not seen as good value for money.

A positive sign is that local councils now employ entertainments officers who are usually given the job of programming summer events. These posts did not exist ten years ago and their existence demonstrates the growth of a market for outdoor theatre. Some of them have realised that buskers' 'competitions' can be a relatively cheap form of local festival for an underfunded council arts department since the performers are paid directly by the public. If the expenses are paid and the public is likely to be sympathetic, buskers will come from far and wide. There is also a move away from public funding; the precedent has been set of a whole street of businesses pooling money to pay for street theatre. However, local groups are no longer nurtured as they were ten years ago. IOU describe one of the effects of these changes.

> We had [during the 1970s] the advantage of being able to devise shows and experiment in the venue. Having no facilities of our own, this was crucial to IOU's development. Young companies do not have this 'luxury'. Venues are not able to give a company sole use of the theatre for up to two

weeks. We never had less than three days to get-in for a show – unheard of today.

The net result is a lack of new groups forming. Often well-established companies collapse because they are expected to compete with their foreign counterparts but are at a disadvantage because of the difference in financial resources available, especially for administration and the increasingly important area of marketing. Outside Britain, there is an infrastructure for the arts which is much more professional because there is more money available to attract those with good management skills. Also, there is the tendency for large British festivals to buy in foreign companies at the expense of local groups. Unlike in France and Spain, there is not an annual festival of outdoor theatre that can afford to present the best of British work. Commercial public relations companies are often interested in using outdoor theatre as an aid to promoting a product or an event. Corporate entertainment demands work that is safe and known, rather than challenging and original. Businesses are often surprised by the fees demanded; they tend to believe that performers are simply fooling about for the fun of it, rather than trying to earn a living. Most entertainers do not mind who they work for but other types of performer often refuse to accept this commercialisation of their work. (Smart costumes and an avoidance of politics are essential ingredients for this area of work.)

Another important factor, in the changes since the 1970s, is that it is now more fashionable to be affluent. Wealth is considered to be a measure of success and outdoor theatre is not regarded as a very lucrative profession. This means that the quality of young talent, which was once attracted to outdoor theatre, no longer goes into the arts or, if it does, chooses areas such as music, film and video. At a more basic level, as Tim Britton pointed out, it is more difficult to survive on the reduced handouts from the welfare state, which had given many artists the opportunity to experiment and develop their work, without so much regard for its commercial viability.

Commercial viability has become the dominant consideration in Britain. For example, work is often designed to appeal to the more lucrative foreign market. The more successful groups seem to spend as much energy in administration, promotion and marketing as they do in the shows themselves. The Natural Theatre Company has developed from a loose co-operative based in a room over a junk shop into a streamlined business organisation with lavish offices and a team of administrators who co-ordinate the five teams which tour world-wide. They were able to draw on their experience with the early video systems to make use of this medium as a marketing tool – an essential element when the format is relatively unknown and difficult to review. All successful groups have been forced to adopt a businesslike approach, although it often fits uneasily with the original conceptions of the work.

At the same time, the general trend in Europe is positive. Gradually there are more festivals devoted specifically to outdoor theatre. More significantly, it is becoming common in France, the Netherlands and Germany for towns to have a summer festival; it is almost a matter of civic pride to add to the quality of life by providing some outdoor theatre. Bringing in foreign companies puts towns on the cultural map. There is a more established precedent of businesses contributing to the arts in Europe, particularly those businesses that have something to gain from increased cultural activity. In Stockholm, for example, the Water Festival can afford to bring in big names such as Pavarotti, as well as a whole range of street theatre. This is paid for by large companies involved in tourism such as airlines and hotel chains. In southern Europe, the warmer weather encourages people to spend more of their lives on the streets. The traditions of carnival have given a solid foundation for the new groups which have become an attractive exportable product. In Spain, the liberalisation of the political situation and the country's economic growth have given outdoor theatre the right conditions to flower.

BEYOND THEATRE

At the end of the twentieth century we can see that elements of theatre have become an integral part of other spheres of activity. In politics, performance is becoming increasingly important; the drama in spectator sports is being enhanced and religion is becoming more of a live event as greater emphasis is put on creating conditions for a spiritual experience, rather than on dogma. The borderline between theatre and reality becomes more hazy as war becomes a media-spectacle. Just as the real world becomes more theatrical, so theatre can move into new areas of performance. The succession of outdoor performers since the late 1960s has been exploring the world outside the concrete restrictions of theatre buildings. They now have the imagination and practical experience to go into many different areas, not all of which could be described as 'theatre', but certainly containing a strong theatrical element.

As has already been mentioned, some groups fit their work into traditional events – Welfare State use Bonfire Night and Emergency Exit made their Santa's Grotto. Patty Bee, the Compagnie Extrêmement Prétentieuse and Phantom Captain have all, in their very different ways, incorporated theatre with restaurant and banquet situations. Theatre can also go into tourism and sports; boat trips and cycle rides have already been mentioned. An educational aspect is also possible; there are already numerous battle enactment societies, ready to participate in historical events. Site-specific journeys could be used as aids for education about the environment and other subjects.

Castles are already being used for site-specific events. At Puy de Fou in the Vendée, France, a site-specific performance is held every year over an increasing period of time. Tens of thousands of people come from near and far to see the show, described as 'the biggest outdoor spectacle in Europe'. Nearly 2,000 volunteers take part in an epic history of the region. The setting is a half ruined château which is viewed across a lake. On the near side of the lake the human drama is played out, following a family history from the Middle Ages through to the twentieth century. There are scenes of celebration, of battle, of mourning, with mass choreography of crowd scenes and lyrical dance pieces. The possible effects that can be created outdoors are used to the full. For one battle scene, a troop of twenty galloping knights do a number of equestrian stunts. At another point, the whole wing of the château appears ablaze, as straw is lit at all of the windows. The lake gives the opportunity to use a complicated array of fountain technology, illuminated by changing coloured underwater lights. Shallow areas make it possible for dancers to appear to glide on the surface of the water. Objects, such as a cross, can be concealed beneath the surface and dramatically raised. Lasers, strobe lighting and projection are also used and, of course, a wealth of pyrotechnics. The show is intended more as *son et lumière* than theatre but it does demonstrate how theatre could be used to promote an area, to convey information about its history (as well as the chronological sequence, old farming methods gave glimpses of social history) and to attract a non-theatre-going public through the use of spectacular effects. There is no reason why this spectacle should not become more theatrical with the use of professional actors or why theatre practitioners could not work within another, similar framework. Other historical locations could easily be used for creation, promotion and education along these lines.

A more modern version of the *son et lumière* is where the *son* is rock music and the *lumière* is in the form of a large-scale, high-tech light show, such as was used at the concert by Jean Michel Jarre in the London docklands. This included lasers, huge mirror balls raised out of the water with cranes, projection on to the sides of buildings and sets of searchlights, some of them at least four miles from the centre of the performance. Rock music has had an increasing theatrical element since the late 1960s. The Rolling Stones use inflatables made by the Inflatable Theatre Company. Theatre artists will do well to fit in with the lucrative rock music industry. There is an increasing demand to 'humanise' discothèques with visual performance. Leo Bassi organises bizarre events in discos in Milan; in Britain, circus performers can be seen at both commercial discos and at the more offbeat 'house raves'. At these, the eccentric performing artists may find they are back in fashion once again. In Britain, a certain amount of live performance has to be included at these events in order to obtain the necessary legal permit. Finally, as already mentioned, walkabout performers are used to 'warm up' mingling crowds at concerts, garden festivals, commercial exhibitions, agricultural shows and leisure parks. These existing possibilities give only an indication as to how far away from 'theatre' these developments could go and demonstrate how theatrical activities could reach into many more people's lives by diversifying into other areas.

THE EFFECTS OF NEW TECHNOLOGY

Many outdoor performers have an aversion to technology. For some the whole purpose of doing theatre outdoors is to find a simple means of expression, unencumbered by the limitations of relying on lighting angles and cues. They also want direct contact and consider that technology distances them from the public. Theatre groups who work closely with the community often aim to demystify the processes of creating theatre in order to encourage others to have a go themselves. They use techniques that are easy and materials that are cheap. As they see it, the more sophisticated the technology, the more the audience is likely to regard the artist as someone 'special' and therefore different from themselves – the thin end of the wedge of elitism. There are some performers, like myself, to whom advanced technology remains an unfathomable miracle, and they have misgivings about relying on technology since it can create more problems than it solves – better to trust the simple craft of acting than have timing and improvisation limited by the whims of electronic and mechanical devices.

On the other hand, there are those who enthusiastically embrace new technological developments. At a simple level, Chris Lynham uses an infra-red remote control device to allow him to set off his explosions with perfect timing. Remote control devices have also been used for controlling model cars (with additions). The variability of terrain outdoors makes this technique perhaps more suitable for indoor theatre. There is also the possibility of remote controlled devices in the air or on water. In Los Angeles there is a group called Survival Research who have made a show with half human, half animal machines that do battle. They have sonic guns that send out a powerful shock wave – in one show they set up a sort of greenhouse and then blasted it, completely shattering it. Lasers are already in common use in large outdoor spectacles such as rock concerts, but their great expense prevents their being widely used in smaller events. Holograms, too, are a possibility, if an expensive one. Les Sharpe of Emergency Exit has been experimenting with the idea of projecting holograms in front of the screen. He is also planning to project moving film images on to a cylindrical screen which is more suitable for outdoor venues where the audience naturally forms a semicircle. Emergency Exit enjoys working with heavy plant machinery such as scissor lifts, cranes, winches and lorries. In one show they had a 60-foot-high mausoleum, with a lift in it, which was built on eight car axles so that it could be moved with the aid of winches. It collided with another part of the set, a house, and destroyed it. In this show they also built a ship on to a tipper truck, using the tipper part as the prow

Figure 19 The dragon in Mir Caravan's 'Odyssey'

of the ship and, as the prow split in two, it became a pair of jaws as well as the image of the ship sinking.

The Mir Caravan had a wonderful dragon in their collaborative production of 'The Odyssey' that was made out of a JCB bulldozer/digger. The head and neck could be easily articulated and it could move forward on its wheels and move up and down on its hydraulic legs. Even back in 1972 Welfare State had managed to obtain the participation of a real submarine in a final sequence near Land's End. Leo Bassi has also employed the military. On another occasion he came across the most expert JCB operator in Milan and organised a show in which he could demonstrate the precision of his skill – picking up and moving raw eggs with the mechanical grab. This type of skill could replace the elephant acts in the circus of the twenty-first century.

Perhaps the technological device most likely to transform outdoor theatre is the radio microphone as it permits the voice to carry much further without the physical hindrance of leads. The increased amplification means that actors no longer have to compete with background noise and therefore can audibly whisper to each other while they move freely over the set, swing on ropes, climb trees, or dance round each other. Les Bubb uses one of these to great effect. He uses his extraordinary mime skills to create the physical illusion of a surreal, distorted world. Using foot switches, he can distort the sound of his voice, synthesising it to extremes of treble, bass and echo, while leaving himself free to move in and out of the audience and all over the performing area.

If this technique becomes slightly cheaper, as is likely, the result could well be an increased use of the voice for both text and song. Up till now, the importance of physicality in theatre has made it difficult to amplify. However, with a wider use of radio microphones, we might begin to see some of the aspects of large rock concerts affecting certain types of theatre. Since there is no limit to the distance to which the sound can travel, much larger audiences can be catered for, the only restriction being on the ability to see the performer. Therefore the visual element becomes diminished as the most dominant factor. Which is, of course, why big rock concerts use large inflatables, lasers and pyrotechnics. The performer becomes reduced in physical scale and is far removed from the majority of the audience. However, if video screens are used in the way they are at rock concerts and big sporting events the activities on stage can not only be seen, but seen in close-up. The intimacy with the performer appears to be restored except that the performer can relate to the crowd only as one body, not as individuals. Neither can the audience choose what it looks at, although a number of images from different angles and distances are often presented simultaneously.

THE MEETING PLACE

On the scale just described, one would think that there was almost no difference from watching a film; at many large concerts it is virtually impossible to see much of what is happening onstage, except by means of the video relay. However, the fact that it is a live event means that interaction between performer and audience is possible, however limited. Rock performers are obliged to use the call-and-answer technique in order to keep that interaction going. The shared response of a vast crowd is a powerful uniting force. It is the attraction of watching a football match, attending a political rally, or being part of a religious congregation. It is not dissimilar to the tribal cry, the gaining of strength and security through a display of unity.

A consequence of the growth of TV, film and video is the distancing of performer from public and the public from each other. With the arrival of film there could be no interaction between performer and spectator but at least the audience shared the experience in the same space at the same time. With the coming of television the audience was separated into the spectators' own homes but even then the event was shared, not in space but in time; 'Did you see that programme last night?' Now that we have video libraries, watching a performance has become a very solitary activity, so it is not surprising that when street performers draw together these alienated individualists to share and play there is a warm response. As more choices become available to members of society, individuality is bound to increase and the old cohesive structures of family, neighbourhood, church and state, will loosen their hold over people.

In this context, the role of those who bring people together to share on a temporary basis becomes ever more important. This is true not only in the sense of 'meeting the neighbours' (although this is obviously of increasing importance), but also on a global scale. Outdoor theatre is gradually being seen as one of the best types of cultural exchange; its emphasis on visual rather than verbal communication eases language problems and is therefore more universal in its appeal. Because it tends to be fairly mobile, it can more easily be transported on planes and perform in places that are without theatre facilities; therefore it is able to travel further away from its cultural origins. Finally it can make direct cultural interaction possible if it uses audience participation. By transcending language and other cultural differences it looks forward to creative contact between ordinary human beings all over the world.

It is perhaps unwise to surmise too much about the future. During the course of this research I have come across books about Performance Art and Political Theatre, written during their heyday, that now seem like epitaphs; so perhaps writing about a subject, classifying it and analysing it, is the beginning of the end. Happily I know that many street artists do not read books, they derive ideas from elsewhere. Recent reports from New York describe break-dancers collaborating with rap artists.

The rapper narrates a simple story about drug dealers, police and gang warfare while the dancers do the stylised actions, resulting in a totally new form of mini-drama with communicator tendencies. I don't suppose they would care much for, or much about, my definition.

Relevant reading

Very little has been written about outdoor theatre. The following list is confined to books that are relevant to the subject and
reasonably easy to find.

Barba, Eugenio (1987) *Beyond the Floating Islands*, PAJ Publications.
Barbour, Sheena (ed.) (1991) *British Performing Arts Yearbook*, London,
    Rhinegold Publishers.
Boal, Augusto (1979) *Theatre of the Oppressed*, London, Pluto Press.
Coult, Tony and Kershaw, Baz (eds) (1983) *Engineers of the Imagination –
    The Welfare State Handbook*, London, Methuen.
Craig, Sandy (ed.) (1980) *Dreams and Constructions – Alternative Theatre in
    Britain*, Ambergate, Derbyshire, Amber Lane Press.
Fo, Dario (1991) *Tricks of the Trade*, London, Methuen.
Frost, Anthony and Yarrow, Ralph (1990) *Improvisation in Drama*,
    London, Macmillan.
Goldberg, Rose Lee (1980) *Performance Art*, London, Thames &
    Hudson.
Heilpern, John (1977) *The Conference of the Birds: The Story of Peter Brook
    in Africa*, London, Faber & Faber.
Henri, Adrian (1974) *Environments and Happenings*, London, Thames &
    Hudson.
Itzin, Catherine (1980) *Stages in the Revolution*, London, Eyre Methuen.
Le Goliath – Guide des Arts de la Rue, Lieux Publics, Centre National
    de Création pour Arts de la Rue, 16 rue de Condorcet, 13016
    Marseilles, France.
McGillivray, David (ed.) (1991–2) *British Alternative Theatre Directory*,
    Conway McGillivray.
Merin, Jennifer and Burdick, Elisabeth B. (1980) *International Directory
    of Theatre, Dance and Folklore Festivals*, London, Greenwood Press.
Nuttall, Jeff (1979) *Performance Art*, Vol. 1, *Memoirs*, and Vol. 2, *Scripts*,
    London, John Calder.
Richter, Hans (1965) *Dada – Art and Anti-Art*, London, Thames &
    Hudson.

Taylor, Rogan (1985) *The Death and Resurrection Show*, London, Anthony Blond.

Magazines and periodicals

Another Standard, *Performance*, *Theatre Quarterly* and *New Theatre Quarterly*.

Index